THE GREAT
AMERICAN
FOOT RACE

THE GREAT
AMERICAN

BALLYHOO FOR THE

FOOT RACE

BUNION DERBY!

ANDREW SPENO

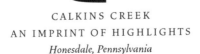

CALKINS CREEK
AN IMPRINT OF HIGHLIGHTS
Honesdale, Pennsylvania

For information about permission to reproduce selections from this book, please contact permissions@highlights.com.

Calkins Creek
An Imprint of Highlights
815 Church Street
Honesdale, Pennsylvania 18431
Printed in the United States of America

ISBN: 978-1-62979-602-4

Library of Congress Control Number: 2016951179

First edition

10 9 8 7 6 5 4 3 2 1

Designed by Barbara Grzeslo
Production by Sue Cole
Titles set in Aachen Std Bold
Text set in Frutiger LT Std 55

For Brian:

small steps,

even stumbles,

but *relentless*

forward progress

CONTENTS

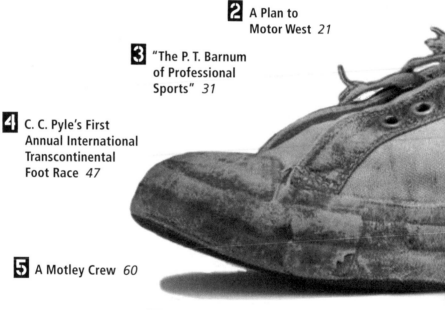

$TART

Boom!

A buzz of excitement filled the air on the opening day of C. C. Pyle's First Annual International Transcontinental Foot Race. Thousands of spectators surrounded the track at Ascot Motor Speedway outside Los Angeles. Tens of thousands more lined the road leading out of town. No matter where they stood, the crowds sensed that they were about to witness history.

Inside the Ascot oval, one man commanded the scene. Six-foot-two inches tall and broad-shouldered, Charles Cassius "C. C." Pyle literally stood out above the rest. Normally stylish, he was dressed casually for the outdoor athletic event. He wore an ordinary tweed flat cap and a simple knit sweater, no bow tie to be seen. Yet Pyle couldn't resist at least one nod to fashion: he had laced up leather boots all the way to his knees. Lifting a megaphone, the Director General, as he called himself, barked instructions to the assembled athletes.

These were distance runners about to take part in "the greatest, most stupendous athletic accomplishment in all history," as Pyle had put it. Not that they all looked the part. Their bodies came in many shapes and sizes: the tall and the small, the thick and the thin, the young and the old. (The youngest was just fifteen; the oldest all of sixty-three.) Their skin

◀ Director General C. C. Pyle gives commands from the sidelines.

9

▼ Led by a small marching band, the transcontinental foot racers march onto Ascot Motor Speedway before a crowd of hat-wearing sports fans.

came in many shades of light and dark, though all would darken considerably in the coming weeks under the glare of the sun. They spoke more than a dozen languages. They hailed from twenty different countries and thirty different U.S. states.

In the training days leading up to the start, one runner had been known to wear a business suit on the track, looking fit to run a bank, not a foot race. Another had dressed in flowing biblical robes, as if he had just walked off a movie set in nearby Hollywood. (He had.) A scruffy teenager with a ukulele strapped to his back and two mangy dogs in tow had wandered into the training grounds making noises about joining the race as an unofficial entrant. (He tried.)

But today, every runner was spiffed up in clean white athletic wear, including a racing singlet that read: "C. C. Pyle's L.A. to N.Y. race."

The 199 registered runners lined up on the track in ten rows, ready to begin a 3,400-mile race that would take them all the way from Los Angeles to New York City on the power of their own legs. They would run an average of forty miles a day, every day, for the next eighty-four days. Nothing like it had ever been tried in the history of the world. Would the athletes hold out? Could their bodies take the punishment? No one knew for sure, but they did know that Pyle had promised $25,000 to the runner who could get there first. This was a fortune in 1928, enough money to give a young man a good start in life: pay for college, a new automobile, and a modest-sized house. Enough for a working man to give his kids a decent education and a fresh start in life.

One hundred ninety-nine men. One goal.

Boom! The cherry bomb that signaled the start of the race exploded. C. C. Pyle's First Annual International Transcontinental Foot Race had begun!

I
THE AGE OF
BALLYHOO

We are living in a fast age,
and the professional athlete who is willing to sacrifice
his bones and gore on the altar of a highly seasoned sport
is the man of the hour in his line.

—Bill Pickens, sports promoter

The year was 1928. The height of the Roaring Twenties. A time of optimism, when increasing numbers of Americans had money to spend and more leisure time in which to spend it. It was the Age of Ballyhoo. A time of excess, when publicity-seeking Americans tried to top each other with ever more outrageous stunts.

Dance marathoners gyrated on gymnasium floors for days on end. Alma Cummings started things off in the spring of 1923 when she danced twenty-four hours straight . . . and three more for good measure. Over the next three manic weeks, endurance dancers extended the record nine times to ninety hours—almost four full days. Most of the record-setters were young women who danced alone and with unscheduled pauses for bathroom breaks. But, as the decade progressed, partner dancing became the norm, and rest periods became standardized and more generous (fifteen minutes for each hour of dancing). Organizers began charging admission for

spectators (the prices went up the longer the marathon continued) and awarding prizes to the winners (anywhere from $50 to $5,000). The turkey trot, foxtrot, and tango were the popular dances, but no special moves were required as long as the dancers kept swaying to the music. In the middle of the night, contestants took turns napping while their partners propped them up. But they would be eliminated if they let a knee or hand touch the ground.

In another fad, pole sitters sat atop flagpoles for *weeks* at a time. Alvin "Shipwreck" Kelly was the first to mount a pole in 1924 and, by the end of the decade, had extended his record from thirteen hours to a mind-boggling forty-nine days! When he needed food or a toothbrush or razor, assistants sent it up by pulley.

◀ The marathon dance is almost over for this pair. The man has succumbed to the sweet temptation of sleep, while the woman struggles just to keep him off the floor.

▶ Alvin "Shipwreck" Kelly sits atop a pole over the B. F. Keith Theater in Union City, New Jersey, 1929. During the course of his pole-sitting career, Shipwreck estimated he spent more than 20,000 hours aloft—1,400 of them in rain, sleet, or snow!

Most important, Shipwreck taught himself to sleep sitting upright with his thumbs in a pair of holes in the pole. If he leaned over while dozing, a tweak of his thumbs would wake him up.

Trained athletes also aimed to go farther and longer. In 1926, twenty-year-old American Gertrude Ederle became the first woman to swim the hard-cutting currents of the English Channel. Trudy, as she was called, covered her body in a thick coating of grease to insulate herself from the 60-degree water as she crossed from France to England. When a storm whipped up and churned the channel into twenty-foot waves, Trudy's coach shouted over the roar for her to come out of the water. Trudy, who was going deaf because of complications from childhood measles, heard well enough to call back, "What for?" and kept on stroking. As evening fell, Trudy followed the light of bonfires and the sounds of noisy revelers on the southern England beach. She had swum thirty-five zigzaggy miles in 14 hours and 31 minutes, two and a half hours faster than the existing men's record. When she returned to the United States, two million New Yorkers cheered her in a ticker-tape parade.

But *twice* as many celebrated Charles Lindbergh the very next year. Lindy, as he was known, became the first pilot to fly an airplane solo across the Atlantic Ocean. For thirty-three hours, he sat in a cockpit so snug he could not stand or even shift positions. For 3,600 miles, he steered by dead reckoning, with only a compass and his calculation of speed for navigation. Sleep threatened to overcome him in the middle hours of his journey, but he found a second wind of energy to carry him on to France. His flight was an accomplishment that made the world seem a whole lot smaller. And it filled Americans with patriotic pride. Four million New Yorkers lined Broadway as 1,800 tons of shredded ticker tape filled the air above their hero.

What feat could possibly top a transatlantic flight? What stunt could create more ballyhoo than an all-American boy accomplishing what had never been done before?

A transcontinental foot race? Possibly.

Some say the idea for the race was hatched at an ordinary Oklahoma City business meeting about the same time that Lindbergh made his historic flight in May 1927. And it was nurtured into reality by a humble highway official by the name of Cyrus Avery.

> Charles Lindbergh makes his way up the "Canyon of Heroes" as New Yorkers empty a blizzard of shredded paper from their upper-story windows. The ticker-tape tradition began forty years earlier as a way to honor popular presidents and victorious generals. In the 1920s Americans began celebrating their sports heroes in the same way.

▼ Trudy Ederle is greased up on the beach of Cap Gris-Nez, France. She wears a two-piece bathing suit of her own design. (There were no two-piece swimsuits or bikinis in 1926.) She found it increased speed and reduced chafing. She used candle wax to seal the wraparound goggles to her face.

BALLYHOO

IN THE 1920S

The word *ballyhoo* can be traced to the earliest years of the twentieth century. It was used to describe a barker's nonstop, colorful talk outside a circus tent. The patter was intended to attract attention and convince people to pay admission for the main event inside. By the 1920s, the word had become generalized to mean lively, attention-getting talk designed to make a sale. Today, Merriam-Webster dictionary adds "flamboyant, exaggerated, or sensational promotion or publicity" to its definition, which is exactly how the word is used in this book.

2
A PLAN TO MOTOR WEST

The American who buys an automobile
finds himself with this great difficulty:
he has nowhere to use it.
He must pick and choose between bad roads
and worse.
—Colonel Albert Pope, "Bicycle King" and
automobile maker, ca. 1903

Cy Avery didn't choose a heroic occupation. He wasn't a movie star, an athlete, or an inventor. He was just an ordinary Oklahoma businessman, but an especially busy one. He managed a 1,400-acre farm, developed real estate, and sold insurance. (Later he would strike oil on his property and operate a gas station and rest-stop café.) He had more than enough work yet always found time to volunteer for public office. Cy saw a need to improve his country's roadways, and he chose to do the unglamorous work of a government official—attending meetings and writing reports—to make it happen. The many highway commissions and associations he served on, usually for no pay, helped make his state—and his country—a better place to live.

> In 1903, before he was the "Father of Route 66," a state highway official, or a county commissioner, Cy Avery was an insurance agent. Yet this photograph already shows the steely resolve he would employ over the next quarter-century to improve his nation's roadways.

THE GOOD ROADS MOVEMENT

Before 1920, most of the roads outside of major U.S. cities were still unpaved, especially in the South and West. In dry weather, motorists choked in clouds of dust. In wet, their wheels slogged through mud up to the running boards. Roads were indirect and rarely went far in any one direction. As one old-timer recalled, "Often you drove 20 miles to advance only 10." Any motorist foolish enough to try to drive across the country knew he had a journey of six weeks or more in front of him.

American roads were *that* bad.

The federal government did no road building in those days, so groups of energetic, forward-looking (and wealthy) citizens took matters into their own hands. They tried to raise money to build private interstate highways, with names like Lincoln Highway, Ozarks Trail, Meridian Road, and Capitol Route. Unfortunately,

these groups of citizens didn't coordinate their efforts. No overall plan guided their decisions. They would reroute their highway simply because another town offered them more money. Besides, the task of building a multistate road proved more ambitious than these highway associations had anticipated. They raised only enough money to grade and pave scattered stretches of road, never a complete highway. In 1920, America's road-map looked like a bunch of dotted lines across the landscape.

By then, Cy had been involved in the so-called Good Roads Movement for more than a decade. In his hometown of Tulsa, his passion for improving roadways was so well known that he was elected county commissioner three times starting in 1913.

Cy worked hard in his new post to upgrade local roads, always with an eye toward making statewide improvements. He organized a "Get Oklahoma out of the Mud Day" to raise awareness and build support for paved roads—as well as for the taxes to pay for them. He gave speeches explaining how good roads could mean more money to farmers eager to get their products to market in the city. He oversaw the construction of Tulsa's first Arkansas River bridge to improve the state's east-west transportation flow and the city's local traffic. He promoted a bond for the county to borrow $1.75 million toward road-building projects.

"THE MAIN STREET OF AMERICA"

Still, Cy believed county and even state funds were not enough. He wanted the federal government to get involved. Cy was pleased, then, when the U.S. Congress passed the Federal Aid Road Act of 1916, which allotted $75 million in highway funds to the states. Unfortunately, the United States entered the First World War a few months later, and road-building projects ground to a halt. After the war, in 1921, Congress passed the Federal Aid Highway Act, which provided another $75 million in funds, this time specifically for state highways, not for local roads.

Oklahoma was slow to take advantage of the new law. (In any case, Cy was busy serving as a commissioner overseeing the construction of Tulsa's all-important water pipeline.) But by 1924, Oklahoma formed a state highway commission and appointed Cy as its chairman. In his first year, he oversaw the paving of three hundred miles of roads and the grading and maintenance of several thousand more miles of dirt and gravel roads. He standardized road signs and the width of all highways at twenty, then twenty-four, and later thirty feet. (Wider roads cost more money to build but were significantly safer.) Under Cy's leadership, the Oklahoma Highway Commission coordinated local county projects to build longer, more direct statewide highways.

In 1925, the American Association of State Highway Officials (AASHO) resolved to do the same at the national level: that is, coordinate state projects to build effective interstate highways. First, the association would establish uniform highway signs for all the forty-eight states. (There were not yet fifty in 1928.) Then they would identify which states' roads would be joined together to form interstate highways. A motorist from Illinois shouldn't have to get hopelessly lost and confused just because he drove to New York or Colorado—or even neighboring Missouri.

The U.S. secretary of agriculture (at that time in charge of the proposed federal highways) appointed a subcommittee to lead the changes. He chose twenty-one state officials from around the country, including Cy Avery. Early on, the Wisconsin representative proposed numbering highways instead of naming them. As colorful as the highway names had been, they were difficult for motorists to keep track of. According to Wisconsin's plan, north-south routes would be assigned odd numbers, the most important routes ending in 1, such as 61. East-west routes would be given even numbers, the most important routes ending in 0, such as 60.

The subcommittee had more power than simply assigning numbers. By approving the routes of some interstate highways and rejecting those of others, it had the god-like power to determine which highways would grow into national thoroughfares and which ones would remain local byways. In the fall of 1925, the subcommittee presented the secretary of agriculture with its map of proposed U.S. interstate highways.

THE LEGEND
OF
ROUTE 66

In 1939, John Steinbeck immortalized what was then known as Route 66 in his book *The Grapes of Wrath*. His fictional Joad family joined hundreds of real-life "Okies" who left their Dust Bowl farms in Oklahoma to seek a fresh start in California. They loaded all their belongings onto farm wagons and headed west on what Steinbeck nicknamed "the Mother Road."

Then, in 1946, songwriter Bobby Troup "motored west" to Los Angeles and was inspired to write a song about the highway. His "(Get Your Kicks on) Route 66" became one of the most popular and most covered songs in American popular music. Later, in 1960, a *Route 66* TV show debuted on CBS. Every week, for three and a half years, the two roving main characters encountered people and their struggles in the towns they passed along the highway.

A novel, a pop song, and a TV show—all three would help transform Route 66 from a mere highway into a central myth in the American story. But Cy Avery couldn't have known this in 1928. The legend of Route 66 was still waiting to be written, and the Transcontinental Foot Race was poised to launch the first chapter of that story.

Predictably, the map contained a highway suggested by Cy Avery. The route would extend between the nation's second-largest city, Chicago, and its fastest-growing one, Los Angeles. Just as important, it would run the length of Cy's home state, Oklahoma, and right through his home city, Tulsa. It was assigned the number 60, and history surely would have been different had it been allowed to keep that number.

But Kentucky felt slighted. It had been assigned no major east-west, zero-ending highway within its borders. To soothe hurt feelings, the chairman reassigned the number 60 to a Kentucky highway and gave Cy's highway number 62.

Now Oklahoma felt mistreated. It was unfair, Cy argued, to ask Oklahoma to change when its U.S. 60 road signs had already been ordered and delivered.

For nearly three months, angry letters rushed back and forth between state capitals. (And all over a *number*!) The chairman would not budge, and Cy looked for a face-saving way out. Perhaps

there was a number with more *personality* than 62? Double-digit
66 would look appealing on a sign. The sound of the double
sixes would roll pleasingly off the tongue. Cy sent the chairman a
telegram, announcing his willingness to give up number 60. But he
added, "We prefer Sixty Six to Sixty Two." And the rest, as they say,
is history.

HIGHWAY BOOSTERS

As hard as he had worked to improve county and state roads, Cy
Avery now put his heart and soul behind his new highway. He
helped form the U.S. 66 Highway Association, whose main goal,

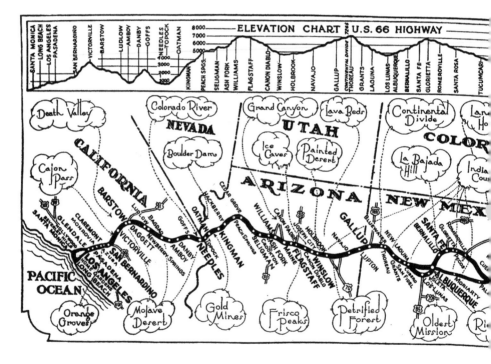

▲ The U.S. 66 Highway Association produced this
map in 1930 to show would-be travelers the major
towns, sights, and landmarks along the way.

28

as one member described it, was to "speed up construction, popularize the highway and promote travel activity of many kinds." This kind of work, which aims to promote business activity, is called "boosterism." Cy Avery and his association became boosters for Highway 66, which they started calling "The Main Street of America."

A slogan was fine, but the association needed more publicity to get Americans—still uncomfortable with the idea of driving their automobiles beyond the horizon—onto Highway 66. Amid the formalities of an association meeting, sometime in the late spring of 1927, a man shouted out a bold proposal: "Put on a foot race!"

The suggestion was greeted by howls of laughter.

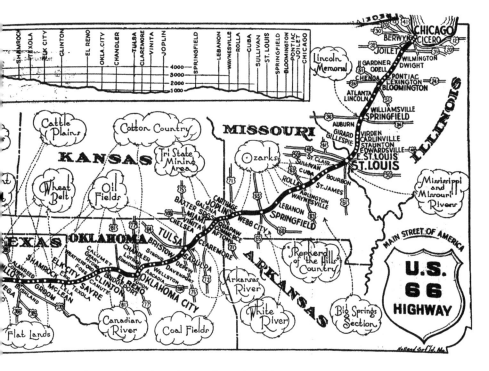

The elevation chart along the top shows that Arizona provided the longest, steepest climb for the transcontinental foot racers.

A foot race from Los Angeles to Chicago? 2,400 miles? The idea was too crazy to consider. When the guffaws died down, the man behind the voice explained that a foot race would allow the event to take place along the entire length of the highway, not just in a select city or two. The runners and their entourage of fans and support crew would bring dollars to the towns on the route and, more important, ballyhoo to the young highway.

The association members warmed to the idea, but they questioned their ability to organize an event as complex as a foot race two-thirds of the way across the country. The man explained that there was a fellow who could. He had, in fact, been talking about doing just that. His name was Charles Cassius "C. C." Pyle and if anyone could organize a two-thousand-mile foot race, it was Pyle, "the P. T. Barnum of professional sports."

➤ Charles Cassius "C. C." Pyle radiated confidence and dressed to impress. Like P. T. Barnum before him, he knew how to put on a good show—and sell it to an eager public.

3
"THE P. T. BARNUM OF PROFESSIONAL SPORTS"

Money meant nothing to Pyle. . . .
He liked to hear his name mentioned.

—Red Grange, football player and assistant race director

What did P. T. Barnum have to do with C. C. Pyle or professional sports?

Three-quarters of a century before the Transcontinental Foot Race, Phineas Taylor Barnum, the man who would lend his name to the famed Ringling Brothers and Barnum & Bailey Circus, had single-handedly invented the art of American showmanship. The glitzy kind. The kind that creates a buzz and gets people talking. Such as when he displayed the "Feejee" Mermaid at his American Museum. (It turned out to be a little-known Japanese art form of a monkey head sewn onto the tail of a fish.) Or when he advertised Joice Heth as the world's oldest woman: 160 years old and the former nurse of George Washington. (She turned out to be closer to 80.) The newspapers called him the Prince of Humbug, which Barnum

In 1851, P. T. Barnum was already an accomplished humbug, or fraud, but this illustration in H. L. Stephens's *A Comic Natural History of the Human Race* helped solidify Barnum's reputation as "the greatest Humbug of them all."

insisted meant simply "putting on . . . glittering appearances" to attract the public's attention. (A lot like *ballyhoo*, in other words.) But most people understood *humbug* to mean a "swindle," "hoax," or "cheat." So being called the P. T. Barnum of Professional Sports was both a compliment and a critique.

How had C. C. Pyle come to earn this mixed reputation?

THE SPORTING LIFE

Young Charley grew up in central Ohio in the 1890s, a time when sports were being promoted as a healthy activity for boys. In just a few decades, the American frontier had been settled and the Wild West tamed. As a result, Americans were concerned that the younger generation would lose the "frontier spirit" that had defined the nation for so long. Could sports take the place of the rugged outdoors? Some Americans believed they could. High-school and college sports could help town and city boys learn the manly virtues of "courage, resolution, and endurance," as Theodore Roosevelt put it, that they might otherwise miss out on.

Young Charley enjoyed boxing, bicycling, and the brand-new sport of basketball. When he was sixteen, Charley found another way to get involved in sports. He organized a race between one of his hometown buddies and Ohio's famed cycling speedster, Barney Oldfield. The outcome was never in doubt, yet somehow Charley found sports fans willing to pay to watch. When Oldfield won, he pocketed a $25 prize, but Charley kept $7 for himself as the event's promoter.

Charley's mother pushed him to attend Ohio State University, but he was too restless to stay confined to a desk. After he turned eighteen, Charley took a job as a traveling salesman and worked his way out West by train. His product—Western Union time-service clocks—didn't sell, even though they kept accurate local time for travelers in the days before time zones. Pyle was forced to find other work that paid. In a Northern California mining camp, he made his second attempt at sports promotion. He set up a boxing match between an aging miner and . . . himself. Pyle convinced the other miners to pay for the live sports entertainment and pooled the proceeds to make the prize money. Winning the pot seemed like a sure thing—Pyle was fifty pounds heavier and thirty years younger—but Pyle had overlooked an important fact: the man was a former boxing champion. Besides, the miner was so stooped over, Pyle couldn't land a solid punch. The fight ended in a split decision, and the two boxers shared the winnings.

THE ENTERTAINMENT BUSINESS

Pyle retired from sports (for the time being) and turned to show business. He worked as the "advance man" for a vaudeville troupe, a traveling variety show, in Northern California, Oregon, and Washington State. Pyle would arrange the troupe's performances and accommodations ahead of its arrival in town. He also filled in onstage when one of the actors couldn't appear, and he wrote glowing reviews of his own troupe's performances for local newspapers.

Pyle also got involved in the brand-new movie business. He managed two theaters in Oakland, California; built one of his own in Boise, Idaho; and even established a film production company in Texas.

During these years, Pyle married twice, and divorced as many times. Finally, in 1914, he moved back to the Midwest and appeared to settle down. He sold movie-theater organs for the next seven years ("silent movies" were not, in fact, all that silent), then made his big move in 1921 when he built a movie palace in the college town of Champaign, Illinois. It did so well, he built four more theaters in Illinois and one in Indiana over the next four years. Then, one evening in early fall 1925, football great Red Grange walked through the door of his Champaign movie theater and changed Pyle's life forever.

STAR POWER

Grange was a tailback for the hometown University of Illinois football team. He had been making a sensation on campus ever since his arrival as a freshman in 1922 and especially since his record-setting performance against the University of Michigan in October 1924. On that day, he took the opening kickoff ninety-five yards for a touchdown and followed it up with three more touchdown runs of sixty-seven, fifty-six, and forty-four yards—all by the end of the first quarter! Huffing and puffing on the sidelines, Grange told the team trainer, "I'm so dog-tired I can hardly stand up."

In the movie theater in 1925, Pyle took one look at the rugged face of Red Grange and saw his opportunity to get back into sports promotion. In fact, in the quarter century since the Barney Oldfield bicycle race, Pyle had never lost his passion for the sports business. And the opportunities for ballyhoo had only increased. Syndicated newspapers, newsreel films, and broadcast radio—what's now called mass media—were making sports heroes national figures for the first time: Big Bill Tilden in tennis, Jack Dempsey in boxing, and, above all, Babe Ruth in baseball. Pyle recognized Grange's star power and knew that, with the right management, he could become just as famous.

Pyle approached the young tailback and made his offer. "How would you like to make one hundred thousand dollars, or maybe even a million?" All Grange had to do was turn pro and sign on with Pyle as his agent.

It wasn't an obvious decision. The National Football League was just a few years old and, as George Halas, its winningest coach, later summed it up, "was pretty much of a catch-as-catch-can affair. Teams appeared one week and disappeared the next." These same teams would sometimes hire college players to play a game or two when injury thinned their rosters. Schedules were loose agreements between teams that could be changed at will. Nor was the NFL in any way "national." Teams came from only a handful of midwestern and northeastern states. At a time when big college football rivalries could attract sixty thousand fans, professional games were lucky to draw ten thousand paying customers.

But Grange welcomed Pyle's message. He understood that his football talent was "God-given," and that it was up to him to put it to good use. If playing football could bring him enough money

▼ Red Grange makes 'em miss in the most productive quarter of his most historic game: October 18, 1924, against Michigan. By this time, the middle of his junior year, Grange is using cutbacks and changes of speed to elude tacklers and extend his runs.

to pay back his father for college and be financially secure for life, as Pyle promised, Grange knew he would be a fool to pass it up. Following the last game of the college football season, six months before he was due to graduate, Grange announced he was dropping out of school and turning pro. He would play for the Chicago Bears.

THE CONTROVERSY

Sportswriters and college administrators were shocked and appalled. One newspaper argued that Grange had "harmed college football" and had "done a disservice" to the school he represented. He was wrong, it insisted, to use his college athletic experience for personal gain. Even Grange's own University of Illinois coach, Bob Zuppke, criticized him in a speech, saying he didn't want any more "$100,000 football players" on his team.

"I'm getting it—in the neck," Grange said, talking about the criticism, not the play on the field. "I would have been more popular if I had joined the Capone mob," he exaggerated, referring to the infamous Chicago gangsters.

Grange suited up for his first Bears game in late November 1925, just five days after his retirement from college ball. He played in eight professional games over the next seventeen days (and would have played in ten if he hadn't sat out two games with a bruised arm). It was a grueling pace for the entire team, like playing half a modern NFL season in little more than two weeks. But Charley Pyle had been right about Grange's star power. Suddenly, fans were paying to see professional football in numbers that approached the college game. In New York, sixty-five thousand paid to see Grange lead the Bears—and twenty thousand more were turned away for lack of seating.

Pyle understood instinctively how fame worked. If a promoter wanted to make his client money, he had to strike quickly, while the ballyhoo was still fresh. So, while Grange was busy dodging tacklers, Pyle hustled to make business connections. In addition to the $100,000 contract with the Chicago Bears, Pyle arranged product endorsements for Grange, including a sweater, a doll, shoes, ginger ale, and even a meatloaf (for a combined $40,000 in earnings). He obtained a part for Grange in a new football movie, *One Minute to Play,* which brought in another $30,000 in income (though Pyle had flashed a fake $300,000 check for reporters to make them think Grange was earning a lot more, and to create some ballyhoo). And Pyle organized what would soon become his personal specialty: the professional sports tour.

Pyle arranged a postseason barnstorming tour for the Bears in two regions of the country that had not yet seen professional football: the less developed South and the distant West. The road trip was demanding—nine more games and seven thousand miles of train travel in less than six weeks—but "wasn't nearly as hard," Grange decided, as the November-December schedule had been. Overall, Grange had played twenty-five games since the previous September: eight with Illinois, eight with the Bears in the Northeast and Midwest, and nine barnstorming across the South and West. Grange felt "in need of a good long vacation."

He deserved it, and he could afford it, too. Pyle handed him a $50,000 check at the end of the last game. In fact, after just a few months with Pyle as his agent, Red Grange earned, or was contracted to earn, almost a quarter of a million dollars. This kind of money for sports celebrities, especially for work *off* the field in advertisements, endorsements, and films, was new. It was 100 percent C. C. Pyle's doing, so he made sure to take 40 percent of Grange's earnings.

AMATEUR VERSUS PROFESSIONAL SPORTS

The tension between amateur and professional sports goes back at least to the middle of the nineteenth century. At that time, working-class men competed for money in athletic contests that were bet on by wealthy gentlemen. In the upper classes, gentlemen athletes formed sporting clubs as a way to socialize in a vigorous, manly setting. As more athletic clubs formed, they developed rivalries. Gentlemanly fair play gave way to a desire to win at all costs. The clubs began paying star athletes from the lower classes to bolster their lineups, mixing amateur and professional players.

Football followed a parallel course. In colleges, where football first took hold midcentury, the sport was praised as a way for boys to develop manly virtues: strength, toughness, and a sense of fair play. Again, the will to win overwhelmed these high-minded goals. Colleges offered gifts and payments to attract star athletes, including those from the middle and lower classes. By the turn of the twentieth century, colleges had become as concerned with the money they made selling tickets as they were about the personal growth of their young athletes. Two decades after that, in the 1920s, college football fans were still praising the virtues of amateurism, even while college football commanded more money than the upstart National Football League.

Tennis started as a sport of the privileged and took longer to attract spectators. Tennis tournaments began charging admission only after 1913, but the money raised didn't go to the players—at least not directly. United States tennis stars Bill Tilden and Helen Wills weren't "paid," but they did receive gifts and sponsorships that helped them afford full-time training and tournament travel.

In recent years, sports fans have asked if college athletes in moneymaking sports like football and basketball should share in the profits—that is, get paid. Though professional sports are now fully accepted, the tension between them and the values of amateurism persists into the twenty-first century.

▲ Red Grange receives top billing for the new football
movie, *One Minute to Play*. The small print in the middle
explains that he appears "by arrangement with
C. C. Pyle and W. E. Shallenberger," a film producer.

Before the start of Grange's second season, Pyle asked the Bears' management for partial ownership of the team, for both him and his client. When the Bears' owners declined, Pyle took his star and, incredibly, formed a whole new team (the New York Yankees, named for the popular baseball team) for him to play on, and then a whole new league (the American Football League, or AFL) for him to play against. Some called it the "Red Grange League," which had some truth to it.

ON A ROLL

Pyle was on a roll. Why, he thought, should he stick to just one sport? Even as he was starting up a brand-new football league in the fall of 1926, Pyle organized America's first professional tennis tour. He contracted the fiery French champion Suzanne Lenglen plus another woman for her to play against and two men to play each other. But Lenglen was the centerpiece. She had dominated women's tennis for six years and, just as important, radiated glamour and personality. The French called her "the Goddess," but some Americans weren't so sure. In her only other match on United States' soil back in 1921, she had pleaded illness and dropped out after falling behind in the first set. Americans accused her of being a quitter. Pyle's friends warned him against signing someone who made a poor first impression, but Pyle saw it differently: "The fact that people hated her was enough for me. . . . People will pay to see anybody they hate." Pyle was among the first promoters to recognize that controversy made the best publicity.

The tennis in Pyle's tour wasn't exciting. Lenglen played the same opponent in all forty matches and won every one of them.

▲ Suzanne Lenglen tracks down an opponent's shot, showing why she was so exciting to watch on the court. One sportswriter described her as all "jumps, lunges and wiles." Even between points, Lenglen would prance around the court on the tips of her toes, "like a cat walking on hot bricks."

But crowds paid to see the Goddess anyway. For their four months of work, from October 1926 to February 1927, Pyle and Lenglen each cleared $100,000. But tensions damaged the relationship between player and promoter. Lenglen tired of the demands of life on the road. Pyle tired of the demands of his willful client. There would not be a second professional tennis tour for Pyle or Lenglen.

THE NEXT BIG THING

In two short years, C. C. Pyle earned a great deal of money and a national reputation, though not always a good one. One of his other tennis clients called Pyle "a con artist, always talking about big things." Sports reporters accused him of "circusing" the game of tennis and joked that C. C. stood for "Cash and Carry" or "Cold Cash" because he was always looking for the next big money-making scheme. Still, people were talking about him, and as Red Grange remarked, more than anything else Pyle "liked to hear his name mentioned."

Grange, who knew him better than most, had it right. In February 1927, Pyle needed a "next big thing" to promote if he wanted to keep his name on the tip of the public's tongue. Pyle's football league, the AFL, had gone bust after just one season. (Americans were barely ready to support one professional football league, let alone two.) His professional tennis tour, though financially successful, was not going to be repeated. What could Pyle do next to keep his name in the papers? What could he do to make a big ballyhoo in this decade of ballyhoo?

Pyle claimed that the idea for a transcontinental foot race came to him in February 1927, just as his tennis tour was drawing to a close. He said he read about a North African courier running ninety miles across the desert to deliver a military message. Could that kind of running be turned into a sporting event? What if the greatest runners in the United States—in the whole world, even—ran a race across the entire country?

Pyle spent the next two months contemplating these and related questions. By late April, he was ready with some answers. He called a press conference with Los Angeles sportswriters to announce his idea for a transcontinental foot race. The journalists filed their reports, some of which were syndicated in papers around the country. That was why the Highway 66 Association member called out, "Put on a foot race!" at the meeting. It was partly a joke, but partly an idea he had read in the newspaper. Evidently, the association liked his idea and approached Pyle about forming a partnership. The members would provide him financial support, if he would promote their highway as his runners ran along it.

It was a partnership of convenience. The two sides had different goals. Cy Avery and his crowd were boosters. They wanted to lure Americans onto their highway to boost business in the towns along the way. The runners, their dozens of supporters, and thousands of spectators would patronize hotels and restaurants, leaving money all along the trail. C. C. Pyle was a sports promoter and ballyhoo artist. He wanted to put on "the greatest race of all history," an athletic event that would get people talking and keep them talking.

Would the partnership hold together? Could it achieve both goals at the same time? And, where would the race finish, in Chicago or New York? C. C. Pyle and the Highway 66 Association were on a collision course. Could they prevent a crash before it was too late? Could the runners avoid being caught in the middle?

4

C. C. PYLE'S FIRST ANNUAL INTERNATIONAL TRANS-CONTINENTAL FOOT RACE

Well, if a man enters a 3,000 mile foot race,
the first thing to examine is his head.
—Unknown journalist

C. C. Pyle set to work making the race what he thought it should be but giving little thought to promoting the highway he was hired to promote. His main concern was figuring out how to conduct a 3,400-mile race, run by hundreds of competitors, taking place over a period of ten or more weeks.

Pyle decided to break the transcontinental ultramarathon into daily "stage races." Each day, he would select a town thirty or forty miles away, which he called the "night control point." The runners would run, jog, walk, or any combination of the three to the assigned control point. As they finished each stage, their times would be recorded in a book by the race's official referee, or timekeeper. (They could take as long as they needed, but if they failed to finish by midnight, they would be disqualified.) The daily times would be added together to make a cumulative, or total, time. The runner with the lowest total time into New York would be the winner of the race.

To help him manage the event, Pyle hired six off-season football players to serve as assistant referees and patrol judges. They would enforce the rules and make sure no runners "accidentally" hitched a ride in a car. He hired former 100-meter sprint record-holder Arthur Duffy as referee. And he signed famed trainer Hugo Quist as his physical director (trainer). Perhaps most important was Pyle's assistant director general, his trusted football client, Red Grange. Grange was the race's official starter, but his primary role was to attract crowds with the star power of his name, which Pyle had done so much to build up.

Pyle sent advertisements to newspapers and radio stations across the country and around the world. He sent Physical Director Quist to Europe to meet with its best distance runners and personally invite them to participate. In the end, fifty-six runners, about one-quarter of the athletes who made it to the starting line, came from abroad, though not as many top-tier athletes as Pyle had hoped. The largest group of foreigners, a total of fifteen, came from next door, Canada. Finland and Germany were well represented with seven men each. Eleven other European countries sent at least one runner, while only four non-European countries did: Turkey, the Philippines, South Africa, and Australia (and the latter two were part of the British Empire). The rest came from thirty different American states, the largest number from California.

▲ Pyle (left) and Grange, director general and
assistant director general, stand before a race bus.
Notice that Grange, whose humble summer job through
junior high and high school was hauling blocks of ice to
Illinois homemakers, has taken on the well-tailored look
of a businessman after just two years as Pyle's client.

A BRIEF HISTORY
OF THE
MARATHON

The first run from ancient Marathon, Greece, was 140 miles. The second one was only 26 and probably didn't even happen. Yet it is the second that has been forever memorialized in the modern marathon race. Why?

In 490 BCE, the powerful Persians had invaded the Athenians on the nearby plains of Marathon. Greatly outnumbered, the Athenians sent a professional courier to their ally, Sparta, to appeal for support. Pheidippides ran 140 miles in two days, but the Spartans dallied. They showed up too late to be of use. Impressive run; meaningless results.

Fortunately, the Athenians fought bravely and repelled the Persians without Spartan support. Then the storytellers took over.

Instead of a run to Sparta *before* the battle, they imagined a run *after* the victory, 26 miles to Athens, to spread the good news. "Hail! We are victorious!" Pheidippides might have shouted. Or perhaps, "Rejoice, we conquer!" as the poet Robert Browning had him declare before falling dead of a burst heart.

The founder of the modern Olympic Games, Pierre de Coubertin, rather liked this poetic legend. It inspired him to invent a new race between Marathon and Athens for the first modern Olympics in 1896. (The ancient Olympics began in 776 BCE and were held annually—and then every four years—for about a thousand years.) The 26-mile race would reflect back on the glory of ancient Greece, and it would create a little *ballyhoo* to attract interest in the games.

The race was so new, only seventeen athletes entered that first Olympic marathon. But enthusiasm for the event spread, especially in America. The very next year, 1897, Boston held the first of its annual marathons. Other cities followed suit, as America experienced its first marathon boom. By 1928, at least twenty American cities held marathons, though with many fewer runners than today's events.

INTERNATIONAL STANDOUTS

Among the Europeans, Willie Kolehmainen of Finland was perhaps the most accomplished. Back in 1912, Willie had set the world record for the marathon in 2 hours 29 minutes, then promptly turned professional. Willie had yet to make much money; there were too few paying opportunities in the sport. Instead, Willie earned a living as a bricklayer and trained in his off-hours. In 1920, he coached his brother, Hannes (still an amateur), to a gold medal in the marathon at the Antwerp Olympics. Now, at age forty, Willie hoped to make his professional running pay. If he could win Pyle's transcontinental trek, he would earn almost a lifetime's wages in a single, admittedly grueling, race.

But first, Willie would have to beat Arthur Newton, possibly the greatest distance runner of his generation. Born and raised in England, Arthur had emigrated from there to the newly formed Union of South Africa, where he attempted to become a farmer. After a series of land disputes, Arthur took his grievances to the government, only to be ignored. Strangely, he thought that winning the Comrades Marathon, a recent event, might earn him the attention he sought. With just five months of training, Arthur won the 55-mile, mostly uphill run in record time. By then, he understood that he had a special talent. Besides, the government kept ignoring his pleas, and his father kept giving him money. So he kept on running.

By 1928, Arthur had logged more than 40,000 road miles, or an average of 20 miles a day, each and every day, for six years! Along the way, he had set the record for every ultramarathon distance in the books (any distance over 26.2 miles), including 100 miles at 14 hours and 22 minutes just two months before the start of the Transcontinental Foot Race.

By joining Pyle's race and competing for money, though, Arthur was choosing to give up his amateur status. Never again would he be allowed to compete in amateur events. Arthur didn't make the decision lightly. But as a runner who trained full-time, he understood that he was not really an *amateur* anyway. Besides, he needed the income. The $25,000 prize Pyle was offering to the winner would help him pay off his debts and gain independence from his father.

Other international standouts included ninety-six-pound Olli Wantinnen, another Finn, and the only slightly larger Peter Gavuzzi of Great Britain. Peter grew up in England with a French mother and an Italian father. He spoke three languages, worked as a chef, and had won a marathon and a 50-mile race. One reporter described him as a "beautifully built little fellow" who ran with "poetry of motion." Another sportswriter resorted to poetry of his own when he said that Gavuzzi "seemed to just glide over the ground as a swallow glides through the air." But Peter had an unusual habit for a distance athlete: he smoked!

AMERICAN MARATHONERS AND COLLEGE ATHLETES

Several middle-aged American marathoners attracted attention. Arne Suominen, a Finnish-American doctor from Detroit, had won the Worcester (Massachusetts) Marathon in 1920. Johnny Salo, another Finnish immigrant and an unemployed New Jersey shipyard worker, was a Boston Marathon winner in 1926—not as an individual runner but in the team competition as a member of the winning Finnish American Athletic Club. Mike Joyce, an assembly-line worker at a Cleveland automotive plant, had performed well in several marathon and ultramarathon events. Mike was an Irish immigrant who hoped a share of the prize

International Trans-Continental Foot Race

Organized and Directed by C. C. PYLE

Open to Any Physically Fit Male Athlete in the World!

GENERAL INFORMATION

DATE OF START from Los Angeles, California, Sunday, March 4, 1928.

FINISH in New York City.

ROUTE OF THE RACE will be over U. S. 66 Highway between Los Angeles and Chicago. Route between Chicago and New York will be announced March 1, 1928. List of control checking points and detailed information will be mailed entrants and supplied to others interested as soon as available.

PRIZES:

To the winner	$25,000
Second	10,000
Third	5,000
Fourth	2,500
Fifth	1,000
Sixth	1,000
Seventh	1,000
Eighth	1,000
Ninth	1,000
Tenth	1,000

IN ORDER to win one of the above capital prizes contestant must finish the race in New York City.

ADDITIONAL MONEY PRIZES, which may be donated by counties, cities and towns along the route, will be awarded the first five contestants to arrive at night control point, where offered, without regard to positions these five contestants occupy in the race.

THE MANAGEMENT WILL PROVIDE, following the start of the race, lodging and food, medical supervision, transportation of a limited amount of personal effects, the same quality of pure drinking water along the route, but cannot assume any other expenses of the contestants. There will be no bonuses, guarantees or other financial assistance given any entrant by the management.

THE RACE WILL BE CONDUCTED in the following manner: The contestants will be started from Los Angeles. Night control points, ranging in distance of approximately forty to seventy-five miles apart, according to the condition of road, climate, etc., will be specified in advance of start. Contestants may run or walk, as they please, the actual time consumed by each between their start from, and finish at, control points being credited daily. Each morning all contestants will start in the same manner as at Los Angeles, and will run daily on the same system. For example, should contestant Number 77 gain 30 minutes on the second contestant each day, he will be started each morning with the field, and although he may be leading the race by thirty hours on the day before the finish of the race in New York, he will be started with the field from the previous night control on the morning of the finish at the same time all other contestants start. This is the only manner in which the race can be supervised successfully by officials.

AT EACH NIGHT CONTROL STOP a commissary and diet kitchen will be established for serving evening and morning meals under the supervision of expert dieticians. Medical and training headquarters will be established also in conjunction with the commissary, where doctors, nurses, trainers, rubbers, and handlers may administer care to contestants. Lunch, drink, shoe repair and medical aid stations will be established at points along the highway daily.

STATE, COUNTY AND CITY OFFICIALS will be asked to co-operate with officials of the race to insure athletes against undue hazards and possible injuries resulting from congestion, traffic and lack of proper police control.

A CARAVAN of trucks, busses, private and official cars to provide transportation for officials, doctors, directors, shoe-repairmen, equipment, newspaper and press correspondents, photographers, motion picture news weekly cameramen, personal effects, equipment, entertainment, etc., will accompany contestants over the entire route from Los Angeles to New York City.

EACH CONTESTANT will be required to deposit in a Los Angeles bank one hundred dollars not later than twenty-four hours before the start of the race, which amount the bank will hold as trustee until the contestant either finishes the race in New York City or is officially declared out of the race. This is for the purpose of guaranteeing the management the contestant will not be without funds to reach home should he drop out of the race. The bank will wire the amount deposited to a contestant upon certification of race officials that contestant officially is out of the race.

THE PRINCIPAL OFFICIALS of the race will accompany the contestants from Los Angeles to New York City and will give close attention to providing comfort for the contestants and will strictly supervise the duties of local officials who will be recruited in advance from among representative citizens in different control cities. Unmarked cars containing officials will continuously patrol the course over which that day's run is being made, and will immediately report any contestant observed accepting rides or assistance or any infraction of the rules.

THE MANAGEMENT DESIRES to emphasize the point that all contestants will be so thoroughly supervised between control points that accepting rides or other unfair assistance cannot escape detection with immediate disqualification resulting.

EACH ENTRANT MUST REPORT in Los Angeles, California, at the official training grounds, for final conditioning for the race, not later than February 12, 1928, and must be willing at all times to submit to a physical examination by official physicians. All entrants must assume their own expenses until the actual start of the race on March 4th.

IT IS THE DESIRE OF THE MANAGEMENT to aid entrants by giving them information and offering suggestions from time to time, and for this purpose a bureau will be maintained at each of its headquarters where all inquiries will receive painstaking attention. These bureaus will be in the nature of a clearing-house for helpful information.

ADDRESS ALL COMMUNICATIONS concerning the race and applications for entry blanks to

C. C. PYLE

Organizer and Director, Vanderbilt Hotel, New York City, or Morrison Hotel, Chicago,

or No. 615 North Van Ness Ave., Los Angeles.

money—$10,000 for second or even $5,000 for third—could give his five small children a leg up in their adopted country.

◀ This part of Pyle's flyer is directed to the athletes, whose gaze would have been drawn to the eye-popping prize figures in the middle: a total purse of $48,500. The fine print below explains the logistics of the race in detail. Near the bottom, it tells all athletes to report at Ascot Motor Speedway for training "not later than February 12, 1928."

Nicholas Quamawahu came out of a centuries-old Hopi athletic tradition, running in sandals or even barefoot, through the mesa-strewn desert of northeast Arizona. Just the year before, he had won the Long Beach (New York) Marathon, and when C. C. Pyle organized a warm-up race during the training weeks, Nicholas came in first and won several hundred dollars in prize money.

Many entrants to the Transcontinental Foot Race were former high-school or college athletes looking to cash in on their talents. Ed Gardner starred on the track team while attending Tuskegee Institute in Alabama. Founded in the 1880s, Tuskegee was an industrial training school for African Americans. Ed earned an engineering degree and returned to Seattle. He found a job as an underpaid steam engineer and continued to compete on the track in his spare time. He won three 10-mile state championships in the mid-1920s. Though a middle-distance runner rather than a true marathoner, Ed believed he could adjust his approach and at least place in Pyle's race. He told reporters a different story. His wife, Mabel, he said, was tired of all his running trophies cluttering up their home. Trophies couldn't put food on the table or pull their family into the middle class. She wanted to see Ed get his hands on the $25,000, or even the $10,000 second prize, to help advance their family. "Here's a chance to get what we need," Mabel reportedly

55

had said. That was why Ed later told a sportswriter, "My wife pushed me into this race," which was only half true.

Twenty-three-year-old Paul "Hardrock" Simpson earned his nickname for being as "hard as a rock" while playing every minute of every game on his Burlington, North Carolina, high-school football team. Hardrock hoped a good showing in the Transcontinental Foot Race would help him finish paying for college at Elon University, where he was captain of the cross-country team. But to enter the race, he needed $25 for the entry fee and $100 for the travel deposit. (A travel deposit was to guarantee that each runner had enough money to return home at the end of the race or if he dropped out midcontinent.)

Most of the race entrants were forced to borrow from family, friends, or wealthy community members, but Hardrock had a unique opportunity. A local promoter, in the style of C. C. Pyle himself, organized a 500-mile road race between Hardrock and a pony named Maud. Interested locals put up money on their favorite competitor, and the winner would take home $500. Hardrock led much of the way but agreed to bow out when a doctor diagnosed blood poisoning in his blistered, swollen big toe. The pony was on its last legs, too, but it was five miles ahead when the race was called. Hardrock won no money, but he did win the admiration of his fellow North Carolinians.

These admirers helped Hardrock gather the funds to enter Pyle's race, just not enough for a train ticket to get there. Hardrock did what any young man with big dreams and a small wallet would do. He hitchhiked. It took him ten different rides to make just the first 70 miles! And when car traffic slowed to a trickle in Texas, Hardrock had to hoof it across the rest of the state on foot. It took him almost a full month to reach Los Angeles.

Twenty-year-old Andy Payne was a high-school state champion in the mile and half mile from small-town Foyil, Oklahoma. Part Cherokee, Andy seemed to have running in the blood. As a youngster, he chose to run the two miles to his one-room schoolhouse rather than ride the pony his parents had given him. As a teenager, he ran more than four miles to get to high school. To raise the $125 in entrance fees, Andy sought financial support from business groups in Oklahoma City and Tulsa, but was turned down. Andy's father, "Doc" Payne, was a farmer, not a doctor. He saw Andy getting up at 4:00 a.m.—to run, not to do chores—and realized his son's heart was not in farming. Doc Payne approached the chamber of commerce of nearby Claremore and convinced the members to back his son. Better to let him get the whole, crazy cross-country thing out of his system, Doc Payne thought.

Andy believed he was good enough to win Pyle's race and help his parents through hard times. "It's the mortgage I am thinking of," he said, meaning that he wanted to pay off the loan his parents owed on their farm. He added, "I can accomplish in three months what it will take years to do otherwise." But Andy had other reasons, too. He had fallen for his high-school math teacher, Vivian Shaddox (she was the same age he was) but needed money to be able to propose marriage. A strong showing in the race would have the added benefit of impressing his would-be bride.

* * *

The Transcontinental Foot Race had a full complement of runners entered, but how would the competition unfold? Could the high-school athletes stay with the marathon champions for 3,400 miles? Could the marathon champions compete with the international superstars? Above all, what would happen to the motley crew of starry-eyed dreamers who made up the bulk of the field?

Herewith is reproduction of 24-sheet stand (112 inches high and 244 inches wide), lithographed in six colors (the accompanying cut shows but two colors), and available at cost to out-door advertisers, merchants' organizations, Chambers of Commerce, and others, for the purpose of advertising on bill-boards in their surrounding territory, to attract thousands of people for bargain sales day on the date that the trans-continental runners arrive in the respective towns and cities on the U S 66 Highway.

A full line of highly-colored lithographed advertising paper, including window cards and hangers, one, three and eight sheets, and mats and photographs for newspaper advertising, will be available also for free distribution through proper channels.

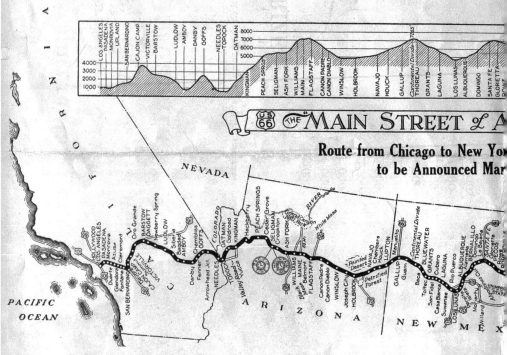

▲ This flyer aims to sell the Transcontinental Foot Race to Highway 66 towns. It claims the event will attract "millions of persons" to view "the titanic struggle" about to be waged on the highway. Probably printed

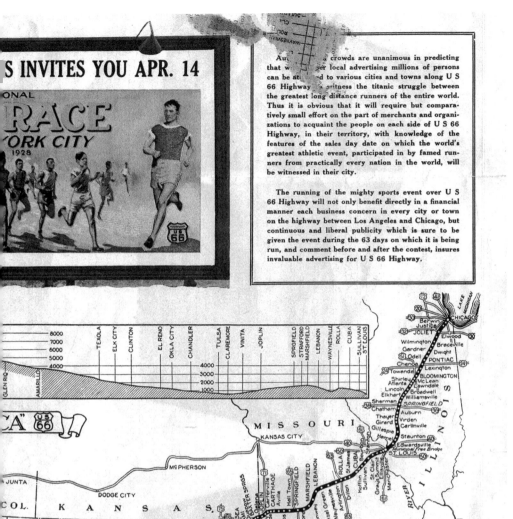

in 1927, the flyer advertises a Los Angeles-to-Chicago race, over sixty-three days, indicating that Pyle was not yet ready to announce his full *transcontinental* intentions.

5
A MOTLEY CREW

I'm here to say it's a motley crew. . . .
The country has never seen anything like it.
—Barney Oldfield, cyclist and early racecar driver

Most of the entrants in C. C. Pyle's Transcontinental Foot Race had no chance of making it anywhere near New York City, let alone winning prize money. As the great Arthur Newton, holder of the world's 100-mile record, observed, the vast majority were "unaware of the magnitude of the task ahead of them." They were not properly trained and didn't understand that the race was "a desperately serious affair." For these dreamers, entering Pyle's race was like buying a lottery ticket: the odds of winning were slimmer than the threads of a worn shoelace, but the possible rewards were too great to pass up.

For most Americans, the glitzy good times of the Roaring Twenties remained out of reach, something they saw only on billboards, in magazines, or on the faces of well-dressed couples stepping out of shiny automobiles. Their best hope of sharing in the plenty was to win a big cash prize like the one Pyle was offering. Most of those drawn to the Transcontinental Foot Race came from the working class: laborers, factory workers, cooks, bank clerks, night watchmen, fishermen, truck drivers, prize fighters, and wrestlers. A share of Pyle's $48,500 purse could mean an escape from the demands of physical labor. It could mean a step up into the middle class—if not for oneself, at least for one's children.

THREE STORIES

Among these dreamers, Hardrock decided that the race had attracted some pretty colorful characters—in fact, "some of the craziest fellows . . . that I ever met," he wrote in a letter home. Each one had his own story, but those of three individuals stand out most memorably among those who left us records.

▼ Soon-to-be transcontinental foot racers compete in what is probably a warm-up race that Pyle organized during the three-week training period.

No story was more inspiring than that of the race's youngest member, fifteen-year-old Tobie Joseph Cotton. Tobie's father was a former auto mechanic, paralyzed below the waist and out of work ever since the car he was working under toppled off the jack and crushed his legs. Tobie had signed up for C. C. Pyle's Transcontinental Foot Race with the hope, however small, of winning enough money to replace his father's lost income. It was a heroic effort to keep his family out of poverty. Mr. Cotton planned to trail the caravan of runners in a beat-up Durant Motors Star Car. He was unable to work the pedals, so Tobie's younger brother Wesley, only thirteen years old, drove the car all the way to New York! (Law enforcement was still spotty on the open road in the 1920s.)

Twenty-year-old Norman Codeluppi had his own surprising story. He joined the race as a way to return to his hometown of Cleveland, Ohio. The child of working-class Italian immigrants, Norman had been sent west to live with an uncle in California, but his heart belonged to a girl back in Ohio. Apparently, it was Norman's plan to run all the way to Cleveland, then drop out and marry his sweetheart, Mary.

Harry Gunn, the son of millionaire railroad supplier F. F. Gunn, had a story as unique as Tobie's and Norman's. Unlike the many working-class dreamers in the field, Harry Gunn already lived in material comfort. He did not have to dream of better things to come. Harry entered Pyle's race not for the money but for the experience of crossing his great nation on foot—walking, not running; speed was not Harry's concern. F. F. Gunn had paid his son's entry fees. He had driven his stylish Pierce-Arrow touring car to Los Angeles in support of his son. He had brought along Harry's sister for companionship and a hired hand to look after the automobile's and his son's on-road needs. Mr. Gunn came prepared to follow Harry all the way to New York. It would be an extended vacation for him, and he planned to enjoy himself.

DIVERSE AND INCLUSIVE

Pyle's race was more diverse and more inclusive than other sporting events in 1928. This was the year before the birth of Martin Luther King, Jr., and segregation was accepted practice. Black and white athletes didn't compete in the same leagues, let alone on the same fields. Yet Pyle accepted all comers (except for women, whom he made no effort to include) as long as they could pay the entrance fees. During the three-month race, he would never segregate black athletes and would even speak out against prejudice on at least one occasion. Two months into the race, at a Chicago diner, Pyle challenged a server who ignored Ed Gardner in order to attend to him first. "Serve the men as they come," he commanded.

The year 1928 also came in the middle of a period of "closed-door" immigration policy. The huge wave of immigration that had washed over American shores between 1900 and 1914 brought more than 13 million newcomers. By the 1920s, almost 45 percent of all European Americans were either foreign-born or the children of foreign-born parents. Many native-born Americans feared their country was changing beyond recognition. C. C. Pyle was not one of them. At a time when Congress was passing laws sharply restricting immigration, Pyle welcomed all immigrants and foreigners to his Transcontinental Foot Race. One sportswriter decided that Pyle should be called "the big chef of America's melting pot"—an exaggerated claim, certainly, but not wholly undeserved.

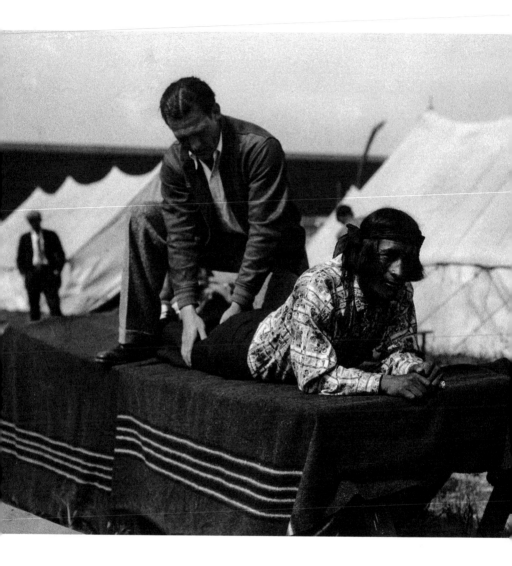

▲ Red Grange gives Nicholas Quamawahu a rubdown, more for the benefit of the photographer than the Hopi distance champion.

FINAL CONSIDERATIONS

But advancing a liberal social policy wasn't Pyle's concern; putting on a world-class sporting event was. With his roster filling up and his daily stage-race concept in place, Pyle realized he might create more drama if he offered a prize for the first to finish at each control point. Why wait all the way until New York to reward the runners' speed and endurance? Pyle announced he would offer a $1,000 purse for daily stage-race winners—not right away, but after the first five or six days on the road, when the money started coming in.

As the early March start date approached, C. C. Pyle had reason to be optimistic. The racers had been filling up his tent city in the middle of Ascot Speedway since the middle of February. Their daily training, especially with the presence of the international stars, such as Arthur Newton and Willie Kolehmainen, had created a buzz around town. The sportswriters in the press were stirring up the ballyhoo. C. C. Pyle's First Annual International Transcontinental Foot Race looked to be on the verge of making sports history.

One problem persisted: the name, which was as long and cumbersome as the race itself. The press went ahead and gave it a nickname that the public readily adopted: the Bunion Derby, the name it goes by to this day.

◄ A bunion is a painful swelling of the big toe's joint, which sticks out of the foot. They can be caused by ill-fitting shoes. Bunions have never been found on people who go barefoot, nor did they occur on the feet of any Bunion Derby runners.

6

LOS ANGELES: AND THEY'RE OFF!

Today the eyes of the world are watching the greatest,
most stupendous athletic accomplishment in all history.

—C. C. Pyle, Bunion Derby race director

At 3:30 in the afternoon of March 4, assistant race director Red Grange lit the starting firecracker and the bunioneers began their 3,400-mile odyssey: once and a half around the motor speedway, then up into the surrounding hills. Pyle had used the newspapers to drum up interest in his transcontinental foot race during the weeks leading up to the event. Now it seemed as if all of Los Angeles had come out to witness the opening day. As many as 100,000 cheering spectators lined the route. Andy Payne later remarked, "You could not raise your head without you facing a camera."

Day 1 was the shortest of the entire Derby, just seventeen miles, and the leaders had no trouble setting a fast pace. The veteran Finnish marathoner, Willie Kolehmainen, breezed through in less than 2 hours, close to a 6-minute-mile pace. Reporters commented that he hardly looked winded, as if he could run "fifty miles a day for the next five years."

The experienced Arthur Newton took a more conservative approach. He understood that the Derby was an ultralong race that required staying power above all else. He hung back at an almost lazy pace and finished in seventeenth place on the day. He didn't seem in the least concerned. He had more than three thousand miles to make up the time.

Ahead of the pack, Pyle had sent a convoy of twenty-five trucks and fifty men. Sixteen tents had to be erected daily for sleeping quarters, as well as a large "big top" tent for each evening's carnival entertainment. The convoy included a lunch truck for the midday meal, mess truck for morning and evening meals, cobbler's

▼ During the training period, David Davies of Sandwich, Ontario, Canada (#124); James Walsh of Walnut Park, California (#210); and a third unidentified Derby runner horse around next to C. C. Pyle's *America* coach bus. Their joking would become less carefree after the start of their three-month ultramarathon. (In fact, James Walsh would drop out on day 2.)

truck for shoe repair, and first-aid truck to care for medical ailments or emergencies. Pyle tried to anticipate the runners' every possible need. It appeared to be an impressive operation (but appearances can be deceiving).

Pyle trailed the runners in a coach bus he called *America*. It came equipped with a kitchenette, lavatory, and pullout beds. It contained a refrigerator, built-in radio, and even air-conditioning, all little-known luxuries in 1928. Pyle was determined to travel comfortably even if his runners could not. His "land yacht," as the press would call it, was said to have cost the same amount he was offering the Bunion Derby winner: $25,000.

THE MONEYMAKING OPERATION

The runners reached the night control point in Puente, California, to find the streets filled with onlookers. Pyle charged the curious a quarter for a Derby program and another quarter to enter the traveling carnival. His vaudeville-like show featured the exotic (Bosco the Snake Eater and Piu the Poison Girl), the unusual (a two-headed chicken and a five-legged pig), and the just plain weird (the mummified corpse of a Wild West gunslinger known as the Oklahoma Outlaw). It was not high entertainment, even by 1928 standards.

Pyle also brought a radio station on wheels, KGGM. He hoped it would stir up interest among radio listeners as the Derby crossed the continent. It would announce the arrival of runners in the evening and their departure the next morning. As it happened, the country's "only licensed mobile portable broadcasting station" permanently parked itself in Albuquerque when Pyle stopped paying the bills. KGGM broadcast out of Albuquerque for the next twenty-five years until it became a TV station in 1953.

Inside the official Bunion Derby program, spectators could find out the names, backgrounds, and accomplishments of their favorite runners simply by looking up their race numbers. They could read about the rules and logistics of the race, too, along with the history of foot racing and current records.

Pyle also lined up corporate sponsors. In exchange for donating their products, the sponsoring companies received eighty-four days of coast-to-coast advertising. Their highly visible trucks proclaimed the importance of their products at every rest stop and control point along the way. Sunkist provided oranges for the runners. Maxwell House supplied coffee. Mobil Oil donated gasoline for the support vehicles. All three—and several more, besides—paid $5,000 each for the right to donate their products.

▲ The Maxwell House coffeepot-on-wheels kept the Bunion Derby runners supplied with much-valued coffee for 84 days and 3,400 miles.

Pyle understood that the longer the race took, the more he would need to pay out in daily expenses—his employees' wages, his runners' food, his vehicles' gasoline. The Highway 66 Association had assured him that he could charge towns along the route $1,000 (or $5,000 for a large city) for the "privilege" of allowing the Derby to pitch its tents on their grounds. Even before the race started, Pyle boasted that he had $100,000 in pledges already in hand. As it later became apparent, this was an exaggeration, an example of Pyle more concerned with ballyhoo than with truth.

Pyle would never have taken on the Bunion Derby if he could not have made a profit for himself. He had become accustomed to an expensive lifestyle since signing Grange and Lenglen as his clients. Fortunately for Pyle, Cy Avery and the Highway 66 Association promised him a $60,000 salary for promoting their highway, to be paid when the Derby reached Chicago, the end of Highway 66. Sixty thousand dollars was enough, surely, to satisfy even the expensive tastes of "Cash and Carry" Pyle.

7
CALIFORNIA: RECKONING ON THE PASS AND IN THE DESERT

*I have never seen so much suffering in all my life
as men have endured on this race.*

—Paul "Hardrock" Simpson, Bunion Derby runner

Willie Kolehmainen maintained his blistering pace on a rainy day 2, but on day 3 he met disaster climbing the dreaded Cajon Pass. He pulled his groin, the connective tissue where abdomen and inner-thigh muscles meet. The injury was so painful he had to drop out of the race the next day.

Willie was not the only one halted by the 3,000-foot ascent through the San Bernardino and San Gabriel Mountains. Sixteen other men gave up before the day was out, though not Nicholas Quamawahu. The Hopi endurance runner raced up the pass and finished first in the stage race—only to pay the price the next day. He hobbled through day 4 with a sprained ankle and withdrew

74

temporarily from the race. Bending his own rules, C. C. Pyle allowed him to complete the stage the next day. He was reluctant to lose a second superstar in as many days.

With Willie out, Nicholas injured, and Arthur Newton still biding his time, Seattle 10-mile champion Ed Gardner made his move. Ed had earned the nickname "the Sheik" because he ran with a white towel wrapped around his head like a turban. On day 4, Ed sprinted down the back side of Cajon Pass and arrived first at the control point in Barstow, California. He notched the first of what would be many stage race victories.

Day	Date	Mileage	Night Control
1	March 4	17	Puente, CA
2	March 5	35	Bloomington, CA
3	March 6	45	Victorville, CA
4	March 7	36	Barstow, CA
5	March 8	32	Mojave Wells, CA
6	March 9	41	Bagdad, CA
7	March 10	32	Danby, CA
8	March 11	57	Needles, CA

On day 5, the Derby began its trek across the Mojave Desert: four days, 150 total miles, 90-plus-degree temperatures, and an unforgiving sun. Cleveland factory worker Mike Joyce spared no words in his assessment: "God, it was terrible. Not a breath of air. Blistering sand, rocky roads, with those mirages dancing up in front of us." Close to forty men dropped out before reaching the far side of the desert.

Arthur Newton drew on his experience running on the dusty roads and in the blazing heat of South Africa's Natal region. While the others wilted, Arthur maintained his pace (though he did suffer a nasty sunburn). Nine-minute miles in the desert heat made him first into the night control three days in a row. By the end of day 8, Arthur had built up a 5-hour lead, and the sportswriters knew no other runner could keep up with him over the remaining 3,000 miles. Only an unforeseen injury could prevent him from claiming the $25,000 prize.

PIT STOP IN NEEDLES

Nestled up against a bend in the Colorado River, below the Grand Canyon, the town of Needles, California, came as a welcome relief on day 8 for the 130 men who had survived Cajon Pass and the Mojave Desert. Those with money to spend could purchase replacement running shoes, a soothing bath, or a hearty meal. The runners had expected to have all their meals provided, which they were. But they had also expected them to be appetizing and varied, which they weren't. The lunch truck provided each runner two jam sandwiches, a cup of coffee or milk, and a small orange. Every day. At night, a retired army cook had the hopeless task of satisfying dozens of different tastes in an under-equipped rolling kitchen. There was no way he could succeed, so he didn't even try. He opened a few cans and served the same bad-tasting stew every night. "Nice, juicy steaks for supper tonight, boys," he teased.

Pyle fired his cook, but he never found a replacement. Instead, he gave his runners a daily food allowance of $1.05, or 35¢ per meal, to use at any diner or inn they could find. When that proved inadequate—"Did you ever try to run 60 miles a day on three 35-cent meals?" asked one derbyman—Pyle increased the daily allowance to $1.50. This was still not nearly enough for men running forty miles or more every day. Mooching handouts became a valuable skill for the surviving runners—at

▲ Arthur Newton wears his trademark "Rhodesia & Natal" T-shirt at an unknown locale prior to the Bunion Derby. Newton lived in Rhodesia and Natal, a province of South Africa.

▲ Climbing Cajon Pass was the first real test the Derby
runners faced. It would not be their last.

least those who, unlike Harry Gunn and several others, did not have a father or a sponsor to help them pay for extra calories.

Pyle had been happy to reach the "civilization" of Needles, too. There he had found more business for his official programs and big-top carnival than he had in the tiny Mojave Desert towns. He understood, too, that the Derby was headed into two of America's newest and least populated states, Arizona and New Mexico. He would find few paying customers over the next three and a half weeks. Besides, he had already lost one-third of his contestants, almost seventy runners. At the rate things were going, the sportswriters wondered whether there would be any runners left when the caravan reached Chicago.

WORLD'S GREAT
DISTANCE-RUNNING
ANIMALS

The cheetah is the fastest land animal, but only for a few seconds. Extend the race ten or fifteen minutes and North America's pronghorn antelope gets the honors. Allow several hours of running and only a handful of animals remain in the competition: among them, horses, wolves, and humans.

In early prehistory, humans were neither fast nor strong, yet they had the ability to travel exceptionally long distances. While their four-footed prey had to stop every so often to pant, the humans' cooling system—sweating!—allowed them to keep running without overheating. Humans quite literally ran their prey into the ground.

Humans lost the need for running when they settled down on farms beginning about 12,000 years ago. But the urge to run never completely disappeared. The ancient world is full of examples of long-distance military messengers, such as Pheidippides, and of endurance races fifty or one hundred or two hundred miles long. Today, the popularity of marathon racing is a testament to our running past. So, too, is the existence of the Tarahumara Indians of northern Mexico.

Often called the Running People, the Tarahumara regularly run fifty miles or more over mountainous terrain. Tarahumara children grow up playing *rarajípari*, a running game in which teams of runners advance a wooden ball around a course by flipping it with their feet. These games can last anywhere from an hour to many hours—even two days!

The Tarahumara are a shy people, but occasionally they have been lured north of the border to enter American races. In 1927, as he planned his race, C. C. Pyle expected at least one Tarahumara Indian to sign up and probably win. None did. Most likely, they were scared off by the ballyhoo!

8

ARIZONA AND NEW MEXICO: ROCKY MOUNTAIN HIGHS ... AND LOWS

We were always a cheery lot
and made a joke of our troubles as we met them.
—Arthur Newton, Bunion Derby runner

Crossing the Colorado River and a state border did not mean the runners' trials were over. It did mean that the Bunion Derby was climbing again: up a winding, rocky Highway 66 into the Arizona highlands and up toward the Continental Divide in New Mexico—4,800 feet above sea level on day 11, 5,800 feet above sea level the next day, 6,800 feet above the day after that, reaching 7,400 feet above sea level on day 14. The air thinned. Runners struggled to fill their lungs with oxygen.

▲ The rocky, twisty path of Highway 66 in New Mexico hardly fits the image of a modern highway. On such a road, bunioneers risked turning an ankle and had to stop every so often to empty pebbles from their shoes.

At night, temperatures in the highlands dropped below freezing. The meager blankets and tents were no match for the frigid mountain winds. And on March 17, the runners woke to find four inches of snow outside their tents, not something they had expected to find in sunny Arizona.

SETTLING IN AND DROPPING OUT

Day	Date	Mileage	Night Control
9	March 12	21	Oatman, AZ
10	March 13	29	Kingman, AZ
11	March 14	52	Peach Springs, AZ
12	March 15	38	Seligman, AZ
13	March 16	44	Williams, AZ
14	March 17	36	Flagstaff, AZ
15	March 18	36	Two Guns Camp
16	March 19	24	Winslow, AZ
17	March 20	34	Holbrook, AZ
18	March 21	42	Navajo, AZ
19	March 22	35	Lupton, AZ

The runners in the Bunion Derby were rediscovering that slow and steady wins the race. Whether through trial and error or with the aid of a trainer's advice, the runners were finding their own best pace and learning to stick to it, more or less. At the start in Los Angeles, Andy Payne had split the cost of a trainer, Tom Young, with two other runners. Tom trailed them down Highway 66 on a three-wheeled motorcycle. He coached Andy to run 9- to 10-minute miles, advice that served him well over the Derby's twelve weeks.

Hardrock Simpson had elected not to pay for a trainer; he might not have had the money, in any case. But by Arizona, the North Carolinian was probably regretting his decision. Blisters and shin splints had slowed him to a shuffling crawl. He would have liked the special care a personal trainer provided.

But the support of a trainer was not a guarantee against a setback. Ed Gardner's trainer, a friend with a car from Seattle, gave him encouragement but not the discipline he needed to set a steady pace. Several Hopi trainers helping Nicholas Quamawahu were not enough to keep him from suffering a serious injury on Cajon Pass. After struggling through ten painful days, Nicholas finally pulled out halfway across Arizona.

▲ John Valis (right) of Los Angeles and Andy Payne run past a gas station in western Arizona. The sign overhead indicates the pair are 64 miles from the Grand Canyon.

Even the veteran Arthur Newton, who knew well enough how to pace himself, was hampered by an inflamed Achilles tendon. His ailment was, in fact, not a new injury. Arthur had never fully recovered from the strain of his record-setting 100-mile run back in January. Indeed, he had told Pyle before the start that he didn't expect to make it to New York. He agreed to run the early days of the race to help supply the "star power" Pyle craved, but also to gain experience with a new kind of distance running.

On day 16, March 19, Arthur hailed the "Dead Wagon"—the automobile reserved for injured runners—and rode to the Winslow control point. Pyle probably didn't mind. Arthur had built up an 8-hour lead and was turning the race into a rout. But Pyle didn't want to lose his star altogether. He hired Arthur to stay on with the Derby as its so-called technical adviser. In his new role, Arthur offered the remaining runners encouragement when their spirits flagged, advice when their stride was off, and suggestions when their bodies ached (soaping for blisters, massage for shin splints). Sometimes he simply distracted the runners from their misery by chatting and joking with them. Arthur also adopted the role of runners' advocate when negotiating with Director General Pyle. He pled their cases for improved living conditions and for reasonable daily mileage—nothing over 50 miles.

With the premier runners dropping out, a second tier stepped in to take their places. Young Andy Payne gained the cumulative lead when Arthur Newton withdrew, but lost it just as quickly when he came down with tonsillitis. In the days before antibiotics, Andy's illness was potentially serious, and his Derby dreams, too, looked to be finished. Somehow, he struggled through a 34-mile day and slept off a monster fever on the night of March 20. No one expected him to get up and run the next day, day 18, but he did.

The Finnish-American doctor from Detroit, Arne Suominen, took the lead when Andy became sick. A newspaper reporter wanted to know what accounted for the success of so many Finnish runners in the Derby. "We're a queer lot, we Finns," explained one. "We run because we don't know any better. There's nothing else to do in our country. If we ever started thinking, we'd quit running." Arne would not be the last Finn to vie for the Derby lead.

THE RACE WALKERS ADAPT

The Bunion Derby had attracted a number of talented race walkers. These "pedestrians," as they were sometimes called, doubted that *running* was the way to win a 3,400-mile race. Skilled, highly trained *walking*, they believed, was.

Phillip Granville, a Jamaican Canadian champion who had "won everything in sight" on the North American race-walking circuit, believed he had the athletic ability to win Pyle's race. The sportswriters had been eyeing Phillip even before the race started. They were impressed by his size and his sturdy, well-built frame. Later, after the race began, they called him "one of the most perfect athletic specimens of modern track and field athletics. . . . mowing down the miles" with his "relentless, machine-like stride." It had been Phillip's every intention to "do no running" until he reached Chicago. Then he would pour on the speed and let the front-runners collapse from exhaustion. At least, that was his plan.

Giusto Umek of Italy had numerous top-three finishes in European events that ranged from fifteen to fifty miles. Many of his countrymen believed he had the skill and the staying power to win Pyle's top prize.

Twenty-one-year-old Harry Abramowitz of New York City had learned to walk fast as an errand boy on the Lower East Side. He had shunned streetcars to save money and speed walked his deliveries instead. Harry began racing competitively after joining the Young Men's Hebrew Association, the Jewish athlete's alternative to the Christian-identified YMCA. When he signed up for the Bunion Derby, the YMHA sponsored him, paying his entrance fees and outfitting him with his many race-walking shoes.

Day	Date	Mileage	Night Control
20	March 23	23	Gallup, NM
21	March 24	32	Thoreau, NM
22	March 25	31	Grants, NM
23	March 26	34	Laguna, NM
24	March 27	48	Los Lunas, NM
25	March 28	38	Seven Springs, NM
26	March 29	30	Moriarty, NM
27	March 30	37	Palma, NM
28	March 31	45	Santa Rosa, NM
29	April 1	32	Newkirk, NM
30	April 2	34	Tucumcari, NM
31	April 3	44	Glenrio, NM

But in Arizona, with the remaining runners settling into a durable pace and showing no signs of future collapse, the walkers faced a crucial decision: keep walking and fall farther behind or switch to running and close the gap. Harry Abramowitz, Phillip, and Giusto all made the switch to running by the time they reached Arizona; they let both feet leave the road at the same time. The other Harry, Harry Gunn, chose to stay a true walker, grounded, with his heels leading the way.

A
BRIEF HISTORY
OF
RACE
WALKING

The Bible says God made the world in six days and on the seventh day He rested. When nineteenth-century endurance athletes began setting records for distances covered in a week, they were not about to outdo God. They, too, stopped at six days and rested on the seventh.

In 1874, Edward Payson Weston walked five hundred miles in a six-day week. His feat set off a six-day racing craze that lasted for the next decade and a half. In six-day races, pedestrians circled a track to see how far they could travel in the allotted time. These races were "go-as-you-please" affairs. The competitors could run, walk, jog, shuffle, crawl—whatever it took to keep ticking off the miles. They got by on as little as three hours of sleep a night.

These races became a popular spectator sport,

with fans betting on their favorite racers. An annual championship competition took place each year in New York's Madison Square Garden, with the winner taking the coveted Astley Belt.

Race organizers started a women's competition in 1879, and Amy Howard quickly established herself as the champion to beat. Of her tactics, she explained, "I go nearly all the time in long races on a dog trot, for I can run that way easier than I can walk."

In 1888, George Littlewood set a record that would stand almost a hundred years. He ran-walked a mind-boggling 623¾ miles in six days.

After Littlewood, professional six-day races went into decline, but the sport of amateur race walking came into its own. It became an official Olympic event in 1908 and continues to be one to this day.

◀ Four contestants line up at the start of the men's Astley Belt competition in 1879.

GRUMBLING

Running in difficult conditions—over rocky desert, in thin mountain air, and, on day 22, through a blinding sandstorm—the bunioneers complained that Pyle had not paid "close attention to providing comfort," as he had promised. The $1.50 daily food allowance was inadequate, showers were rare, and laundering was almost nonexistent. The runners' bedding had gone mostly unwashed for three weeks and, worse, was treated as communal property. The bunioneers slept in a different person's sheets each night. One Derby runner explained, "We undoubtedly slept with our heads on one end of a blanket, where some other unfortunate had his sore bleeding feet the previous night."

The tents blew down in windstorms. Their thin canvas kept out neither rain nor cold nor sounds of the "ballyhoo" coming from the nightly carnival big top. These conditions were unacceptable for ultramarathoners in need of a good night's sleep.

So the derbymen grumbled.

And Pyle began seeking indoor lodging for his athletes: a one-room schoolhouse in Seligman, Arizona; an old opera house in Williams—not exactly four-star accommodations, but an improvement over drafty tents. As the Derby continued east, Pyle housed the runners in whatever shelters he could find: horse stables, chicken coops, post office floors, and high-school gymnasiums. Occasionally, he even paid for a hotel.

William Kerr, a handsome, muscular veteran of World War I, received his own comfortable accommodations from American Legion sponsors. Even in sparsely populated Arizona, war veterans came forward to offer William a shower, a home-cooked meal, and a bed for the night. Pyle insisted that all Derby athletes would "sleep, eat, and run under the same conditions"—no special treatment would be tolerated—but he never took action to enforce his own rule. William continued to benefit from the treatment given by the American Legion, and his racing benefitted as a result. As the Derby crossed into New Mexico, William was within the top ten. He was also one of Pyle's most vocal critics. Over the next eight weeks, William earned a reputation, with C. C. Pyle and with the press, as ringleader of the Derby grumblers.

Housing wasn't the only concern of these men. They complained that Pyle had not introduced the daily prize money he had promised. The reason was simple: the money from the towns had not materialized. Why, wondered town officials, should they pay for something their citizens could see plainly enough for free just by standing on the side of the road? Where else was Pyle going to run his Derby, anyway? Out in the desert? The chamber of commerce in Albuquerque, New Mexico, refused to pay Pyle's $2,000 fee for the "privilege" of hosting his caravan. Furious, Pyle detoured around the city, adding 14 miles to his runners' day. With the largest city in the southwest withholding payment, the prospects for Derby income looked bleak—and with it the possibility for daily prize money.

So the bunioneers grumbled.

But not Hardrock Simpson. He never complained, even when slowed to a shuffle by shin splints. While his competitors joked that he should be called Hard *Luck*, C. C. Pyle expressed

admiration for his positive attitude. "That boy has guts, plenty of guts," the race director observed. In a letter home, Hardrock wrote: "The race is doing more for me than anything I ever did. . . . I am getting so I love every man in the race. I am getting so no task looks too large for me." Then he added, probably exaggerating to keep his mother from worrying, "Physically, I get stronger every day, and the miles seem to click off in no time, and I always finish fresh."

As March turned to April, the Bunion Derby approached the end of its third state. For the four remaining African American runners, Ed Gardner, Phillip Granville, Tobie Cotton, and Sammy Robinson of Atlantic City, New Jersey, a new challenge would soon be added to the physical demands of running daily ultra-marathons. As the Derby ran east across New Mexico, the African American runners encountered blatant prejudice more frequently. How would they survive the full brunt of racism they were sure to encounter in Texas?

◄ John Gober (left) of
Moberly, Missouri, and Ed
Gardner jog down a wide,
flat—and still unpaved—
Highway 66.

9

TEXAS-SIZED TROUBLES

I am not thinking much about the money. . . .
My idea is that it would be a wonderful thing to win in this test
of endurance for the [black] race.

—Ed Gardner, Bunion Derby runner

Ed "the Sheik" Gardner had not yet found his rhythm. He had settled into a troubling pattern of blazing ahead for a few days, then falling back for several more after that. The 10-miler just couldn't set a consistent pace for himself over the longer distances.

On day 31, April 3, Ed surged ahead and led the pack into the last New Mexico control point, Glenrio, which was a problem. The Derby was entering Texas, long known as the Lone Star State but recently nicknamed the "Star Klan State" because of the strength of its Ku Klux Klan (KKK), the white supremacist organization committed to denying black Americans their full rights and willing to use terrorist tactics to do it. During the 1920s, KKK membership was increasing, as was the number of segregation laws. When a group of Texas toughs warned Ed's trainer, who was also black, not to let his runner cross the Texas line ahead of Andy Payne, their warning carried a clear threat.

Whether heeding the threat or just taking a recovery day, Ed

96

finished the next stage race in the middle of the pack. A few days later, a different group of hoodlums threatened to set his trainer's car on fire. They may have resented the sight of a black man owning an automobile they themselves couldn't afford. One spiteful Texan more than likely spoke for many when he told a reporter, "They ain't got no business racing niggers against white folks."

Day	Date	Mileage	Night Control
32	April 4	37	Vega, TX
33	April 5	37	Amarillo, TX
34	April 6	41	Groom, TX
35	April 7	39	McLean, TX

Over the next several days, Ed Gardner, Tobie Cotton, and a third African American runner, Sammy Robinson, kept a low profile. Phillip Granville, who considered himself a Jamaican Canadian, not an African American, kept to himself, but his dark skin made him a target for hostility and discrimination nonetheless. The European runners were shocked and more than a little confused by what they called "American prejudice." One European runner reportedly "could not understand the dumbness of folk who would eat the food prepared by a . . . Negro at one of the points where they stopped, but at the same time refused to sit and eat with folk just like him."

A few days later, in western Oklahoma, Ed had a gun held to his back by a man on a mule, daring him to pass a white runner. Ed didn't accept the dare, but he did resent the indignity of having to choose between personal safety and athletic achievement. When he couldn't take the man's threats anymore, he sprinted down the road and never looked back.

➤ Ed "the Sheik" Gardner shows his style on a Seattle rooftop. By 1928, he had already won three 10-mile state championships.

▼ Ed Gardner (center) poses against the Hupmobile of his trainer, George Curtis (left). His financial sponsor, Los Angeles businessman James Akers, stands to the right with his hands in his pockets. A sign bearing Ed's race number identifies the car as belonging to Team Gardner.

SPRING SNOW

Racial tensions weren't the only challenges facing the Derby runners as they crossed the Texas Panhandle, the rectangular piece of the state that sticks up in the north. On day 33, April 5, a spring storm called a blue norther roared across the plains, dropping the temperature quickly and turning the rain to sleet, then snow. The dirt road turned into a slick, muddy gumbo that stuck to the runners' shoes and weighed them down. Icy winds stung their cheeks and froze against their thighs. Andy Payne remembered it as one of the most punishing days of the entire Derby, worse even than Cajon Pass. "I mean, I was really stiff," he said. "I just barely made it."

And Andy was surely glad he did make it. As the Bunion Derby crossed the line into Oklahoma, the state's native son had become the latest Derby front-runner. Again. With sizable towns, including *two* large cities, and a hometown favorite leading the race, Oklahoma offered the Derby the prospect of large crowds for the first time since leaving Los Angeles.

10
OKLAHOMA'S FAVORITE SON

I realized that this isn't a race at all. It's a miracle.

—Bill Witt, reporter

Attract crowds it did. Schools and businesses let out early so citizens could catch the bunioneers trotting through town. Schoolchildren lined the streets, perching on walls or squatting on curbsides. One youngster later recalled his excitement at seeing what he thought then were "the biggest athletes in the world." Another remembered the occasion as "the zaniest sporting event of all times."

So many Oklahomans and newspaper reporters wanted time with Andy Payne that the young runner found it difficult to hold his 9-to-10-minute-mile pace. Andy's father, Doc Payne, who had crossed the state to greet his boy, did his best to handle the reporters. "Andy is hard as nails," he told one. "He's just running easy. He's got some sense, and he won't try to run away with it all the way." When Andy failed to reach the state capital, Oklahoma City, at the front of the pack, the assembled crowd of as many as one hundred thousand was visibly disappointed. When he did reach the stage-race finish line,

Andy Payne shows his determination while running through his home state. For forty days and counting, #43 has been able to make steady forward progress, not too fast and not too slow. In cumulative time, the eighty remaining runners are all at his back.

city officials rushed him to the podium to say a few words. Andy did just that. He said a *very* few words: "Hello, home folks. I'm glad to be back. Hope to see you in New York." The crowd was left disappointed again.

Halfway Point		Hrs: Mins: Secs
First:	Andy Payne	251:51:31
Second:	Peter Gavuzzi	253:21:50
Third:	Johnny Salo	271:05:21
Fourth:	Olli Wantinnen	282:20:50
Fifth:	Ed Gardner	285:58:34
Sixth:	William Kerr	290:14:33
Seventh:	John Cronick	291:38:42
Eighth:	Harry Rea	295:23:51
Ninth:	Louis Perella	295:53:41
Tenth:	Giusto Umek	305:02:01

The press felt let down, too. The "show was a flop," wrote one newspaperman. "There is nothing interesting in seeing a mob of sun blackened runners straggle in miles apart."

But no one was more frustrated by the results than C. C. Pyle. Despite the large crowds, his earnings were disappointingly small. He had failed to fence off the post-race fairgrounds in Oklahoma City, and thousands of fans entered without paying.

Oklahomans kept turning out to the roadside to see their home-state hero. From Oklahoma City to the Missouri border, automobiles lined the highway and well-wishers stood by to cheer on Andy, who, accordingly, picked up his pace. He had always followed his trainer's advice to run steady 9- to 10-minute miles, but on day 45, April 17, he couldn't resist running just a *little* faster for his hometown fans on the road to Foyil.

◀ Bunioneers line up for the morning's start while citizens of an Oklahoma town crowd in to witness the one-of-a-kind event. Ed "the Sheik" Gardner, with the white headband, takes his stance at far left.

Nine miles before Foyil, however, was Claremore, whose chamber of commerce had given Andy the money to enter the Derby. It was also the halfway point in the race—roughly 1,700 miles from either coast—and the hometown of America's beloved cowboy comedian Will Rogers. The famous vaudeville performer had grown up with Andy Payne's father, Doc Payne, and he joked in his national newspaper column, "I felt kind of jealous when I read that someone"—meaning Andy Payne—"had supplanted me as favorite son." His "jealousy" was just pretend. In truth, he was hugely proud of the local boy leading the race. So Rogers wired in special prize money for the first runner to cross into Claremore, and he made no secret that he expected Andy Payne to collect the $250 prize, which he did!

Day	Date	Mileage	Night Control
36	April 8	35	Texola, OK
37	April 9	32	Sayre, OK
38	April 10	50	Clinton, OK
39	April 11	35	Bridgeport, OK
40	April 12	37	El Reno, OK
41	April 13	34	Oklahoma City, OK
42	April 14	52	Chandler, OK
43	April 15	35	Bristow, OK
44	April 16	42	Tulsa, OK
45	April 17	50	Chelsea, OK
46	April 18	52	Miami, OK

THE CARE THEY NEEDED

Andy Payne wasn't the only one attracting special attention in Oklahoma. The Derby's black runners were greeted enthusiastically by a sizable African American community, which wanted to show them

◄ Will Rogers brought the Wild West to city folks by performing virtuoso rope tricks on the vaudeville stage. Then he "started reading about Congress in the newspapers, and . . . discovered they were funnier three hundred and sixty-five days a year" than anything else he had ever heard of. Once he added political comedy to his act, a national star was born.

good, old-fashioned hospitality. They treated Ed Gardner and company to home-cooked meals, warm baths, and soft beds—comforts of home that made all the difference to weary bunioneers. In the town of El Reno, Mr. and Mrs. George Green opened their home to the black runners for dinner and evening entertainment. The local guests pooled their money and presented the party's honorees with $51 to split among themselves. The money would help pay for the food and amenities C. C. Pyle was *not* providing. One guest slipped Ed Gardner extra cash, telling him, "Come in first; I'm depending on you."

Meanwhile, Hardrock received the greatest gift of all: a trainer. For days, he had been struggling to reach the control points before the midnight cutoff. When he didn't, he was picked up by Red Grange in a support vehicle and transported to the night control point. He might have been disqualified, but Pyle had changed his own rules back on day 4. After Cajon Pass, he had allowed the Hopi champion, Nicholas Quamawahu, to stay in the race despite not finishing the stage race on time. Fairness dictated that he allow other runners to do the same. After missing the cutoff, Hardrock and other stragglers were driven to the points they had left off the night before, adding extra miles to their runs and making it all the more likely they would miss the next night's cutoff. And so on. It was a vicious circle, and Hardrock found himself right in the center of it. He might have called it quits, but he wasn't called Hardrock for nothing.

Just when the runner's state of affairs reached a low point, Wesley Williams, Hardrock's best friend, showed up in a Model T Ford. Both trainer and his automobile had been paid for by the Faith in Hardrock Fund, a group of supporters back in North Carolina. Wesley was intent on seeing his buddy through to the finish line.

For the next month and a half, he would take energy food and drink to Hardrock along the road, such as the honey-and-cheese sandwiches and highly sweetened fruit drinks recommended by Arthur Newton. Wesley would rub Hardrock down at night and give him the encouragement he needed to run an ultramarathon every day.

Hardrock's spirits revived. If only someone had sent a guardian angel to C. C. Pyle, he might have avoided the financial and legal difficulties that began piling up all around him. On Friday, April 13, Pyle had a stroke of bad luck; he was sued by a disgruntled former AFL football player. The player was demanding back pay of almost $5,000, the same amount Pyle expected to collect from the Oklahoma City Chamber of Commerce. The lawsuit canceled out the payment, and, once again, Pyle left empty-handed. It was looking as if his Transcontinental Foot Race might not make it across the country for want of funds.

On the other hand, the Bunion Derby was finally beginning to look like a real race. The trilingual Brit, Peter Gavuzzi, had pulled even with the all-American Oklahoman, Andy Payne. As the two crossed into Missouri on day 47, April 19, Peter and Andy were almost tied at 295 hours of total running (and almost 30 hours ahead of the next best runner, Johnny Salo). What could be more exciting than half a continent of neck-and-neck drama?

⬜⬜
MISSOURI AND ILLINOIS: DASH ACROSS THE MIDWEST

Every man has a different method of caring
for his feet and legs. Blister derby
might be a more fitting title.

—Daily Oklahoman

U.S. Highway 66 skirted the edge of the Ozark Plateau in southern Missouri. Where the road had been straight and open and flat for 500 miles, it now had curves and trees and gently rolling hills. The forested peaks of the Ozark Mountains loomed in the south and east.

The two-man race that had developed in Oklahoma became lopsided again almost as quickly as it had begun. Peter had found his stride and pulled away from Andy. He sped up his pace to 8½-minute miles, then 8-minute, then 7½. By the time the two reached Illinois, Peter had built up a 4-hour lead over the 9-minute miler, Andy Payne. Andy was reluctant to give up on his trainer's slow-and-steady advice, but it was difficult to hang back while his rival sped down the road in front of him.

Day	Date	Mileage	Night Control
47	April 19	40	Joplin, MO
48	April 20	47	Miller, MO
49	April 21	34	Springfield, MO
50	April 22	43	Conway, MO
51	April 23	52	Waynesville, MO
52	April 24	32	Rolla, MO
53	April 25	43	Sullivan, MO
54	April 26	46	Hillside View, MO

For reasons of his own, Peter had stopped shaving when the Derby left Los Angeles. Now in Illinois, he sported a thick beard that gave him the look of a mountain man come down from the hills (which, in a way, he was). But then on day 59, May 1, the beard disappeared. Gavuzzi's cheeks were as smooth as a baby's.

Pyle was furious. He liked it that the press had begun calling his new leader the "bristle-bearded Britisher." It made good copy. It gave Peter a personality (maybe even a little controversy) that Pyle could sell to the public. Now what was he to do? In frustration, the director general blasted Peter in a rant that was overheard (and certainly embellished) by a nearby reporter: "What . . . came over you? Here I've been working like a dog, getting things set for a swell Chicago ballyhoo and you spoil my best plans by getting your whiskers shaved just when they were getting nice and flowing and curley on the ends. . . . That's gratitude for you."

Peter claimed that, tired as he was, he had simply fallen asleep in the chair, and the barber had gotten carried away with his clippers. Unfortunately for Peter, like the biblical Samson, he lost his strength with his hair. The next day, he gave up half an hour to his rival, Andy, and vowed not to shave again until he reached New York.

111

Worse than a shorn beard, though, Peter had an impacted tooth that had become badly infected. Eating solid foods had become too painful, and Peter was reduced to sipping broth and sucking hard candy, a poor diet for an ultramarathon runner. It seemed unlikely that he could make it through the remaining 1,000 miles to New York, though Pyle, almost as much as Peter, hoped he could.

◄ Andy Payne towers over "bristle-bearded" Peter Gavuzzi. In Oklahoma, the race becomes a two-man competition.

OLD DEBTS

But Pyle's problems were greater than whether his lead runner stayed in the race. He was still desperate for dollars. The town of Carthage, Missouri, paid less than his full fee, so when neighboring Joplin offered to pay more, Pyle reneged on Carthage (without returning the money) and stayed in Joplin. Understandably, the citizens of Carthage felt cheated and took it upon themselves to get even. When Pyle's convoy passed through their town, they hurled rotten eggs at his support vehicles (but not, thankfully, at his runners).

Worse, Pyle had another lawsuit thrown at him on day 57, April 29. An Illinois bank demanded he pay back $21,000 on a three-year-old loan. When Pyle failed to show up, the police tracked him down and seized his coach bus. They would hold the *America* for as long as it took Pyle to pay back the loan. That wasn't going to happen anytime soon. Pyle was short on cash, and the Derby wasn't bringing in enough money.

While Pyle worked out his legal problems, Red Grange assumed command of the Derby. The lead runners worried there would be no prize money for them in New York—*if* the race made it there at all. Sixty days and 2,400 miles were looking to be a wasted effort.

Fortunately, Harry Gunn's millionaire father, F. F. Gunn, heard the concerns and stepped in to save the Derby. Traveling with the runners the previous two months, Gunn had become deeply invested in their race—and in his son finishing it. He thought the Derby a fine show, even while criticizing Pyle's "loose" business methods. Though there is no record of what happened next, it is likely that Gunn met with Pyle and made him an offer. Gunn would provide Pyle with financial support in exchange for control of Derby operations. As part of the deal, Pyle agreed to say nothing to the press. Gunn wanted his business dealings with Pyle to remain hush-hush. Later, when asked directly by a reporter, Gunn denied any involvement, saying, "I am not connected with the run. . . . I am not C. C. Pyle's financial angel."

On day 62, May 4, Pyle reached a deal with law enforcement, too. He would retrieve his so-called land yacht by paying just $5,000 on the loan. Pyle rejoined the Derby not as director but as an advance man, the job he had first learned on the West Coast vaudeville circuit. Pyle traveled ahead to make arrangements with the night control towns, and F. F. Gunn took charge of the more important decisions.

Gunn's first decision as the Derby's new director was to rope off the finish line each day. Runners would cross the tape underneath a large circus tent. To enter, curious spectators would have to pay a quarter. Second, there would be no more 30- to 40-mile days. Fifty- to 60-mile days would bring the Derby into New York a few days sooner. Fewer days meant fewer expenses. Finally, the midnight deadline would be strictly enforced. Anyone who couldn't make the control point by that time would collect his deposit and go home. Fewer runners; fewer expenses.

THE END OF ONE ROAD

The Bunion Derby charged into the city of Chicago on day 63, May 5, and was greeted by enthusiastic crowds along Michigan Avenue. None were more enthusiastic than the fans of Ed Gardner, whose performance was becoming a source of African American pride and hope. In an age of humiliating racial segregation and discrimination—where in Texas blacks were banned from even standing in the same lines as whites at the post office, and where in Chicago a black boy who accidentally crossed onto the white side of a beach set off a deadly race riot—Ed's athletic performance in the Derby was proving that a black man was as strong and talented as any white man. He was not the first black athlete to carry the hopes and pride of his people, nor would he be the last. But in the spring of 1928, he was certainly the man of the moment. The Chicago crowd took special delight when tap-dancing legend Bill "Bojangles" Robinson stepped out of the crowd and paced the Sheik down the street . . . with his trademark *backward* running.

Day	Date	Mileage	Night Control
55	April 27	28	East St. Louis, IL
56	April 28	43	Staunton, IL
57	April 29	44	Virden, IL
58	April 30	26	Springfield, IL
59	May 1	32	Lincoln, IL
60	May 2	35	Normal, IL
61	May 3	35	Pontiac, IL
62	May 4	59	Joliet, IL
63	May 5	43	Chicago, IL

The Derby had reached the end of U.S. Highway 66 and would soon begin its march to New York City through the more densely populated eastern states. The raucous crowds of the country's second-largest city made the moment feel like a celebration, though the runners still had 1,000 miles to run. The festive atmosphere quickly turned somber when a car struck the lightweight Finn, Olli Wantinnen. Olli was able to get up and hobble to the finish, but doctors diagnosed a fractured rib. The lead runners realized that their chances at prize money could be erased in an instant if they were to suffer a similar fate.

> Olli Wantinnen, the ninety-six-pound Finn, strides into Chicago, making good time. Unfortunately, his days with the Bunion Derby are about to be brought to a premature end by a reckless driver.

Adding insult to Olli's injury, the Highway 66 Association refused to pay Pyle the $60,000 it had promised him. The group believed he had done more to promote himself and his runners than the highway and the towns along the way, as the contract required. By naming the event C. C. Pyle's International Transcontinental Foot Race, the association argued, Pyle had broken his contract. The group didn't owe him a cent. Pyle never challenged the association's decision. He never countersued for payment.

With their differing goals for the race, C. C. Pyle and the Highway 66 Association had collided in Chicago as expected. Pyle bore the worst of it. The association held on to its money, and Pyle teetered on the brink of bankruptcy. Without a last-minute rescue by F. F. Gunn, he and the Bunion Derby would have stalled out in Chicago. The caravan continued its marathon slog east, with F. F. Gunn in charge and C. C. Pyle as the advance man. Would the new management mean any changes for the runners over the last 1,000 miles?

◄ (Left to right) Andy Payne, John Cronick of Saskatoon, Saskatchewan, Canada, and William Kerr of Minneapolis pick up the pace before a curious Chicago crowd.

12
INDIANA AND OHIO: THE BUNION DERBY ON LIFE SUPPORT

The trouble with Pyle's race is that it's too long
to be taken seriously. . . . A race that goes on for
months and months becomes, to the people in general,
a thing of humor and the butt of many jokes.

—Bill Witt, reporter

Most of the sixty-odd men still competing in the Bunion Derby were no longer running for the money. Only the top eleven runners were still in contention for a prize. The rest were hundreds of hours—days, even weeks—behind the lead runners. These men were running to finish what they had started. They were running for pride.

There was nothing, save a race-ending injury, that could keep them from reaching the Big Apple, as New York City had recently been dubbed by—who else?—a sportswriter. John J. FitzGerald called the city the "Big Apple" for being the biggest prize on the horse-racing circuit.

On the other hand, staying in the foot race didn't require actual *racing*. A few slackers—"tourists," Pyle called them—exhibited no great concern for speed. Veteran Indiana boxer and distance runner Mike Kelly was one. He resented Pyle's treatment of the bunioneers and decided to turn the Derby into an all-expenses-paid cross-country vacation. Kelly earned the nickname "bridge sleeper" for his habit of catching a few z's under trestles and overpasses. But as the race approached Goshen, Indiana, on day 66, May 8, the other runners agreed—in what was becoming a Derby tradition—to let the local boy lead the way into his hometown. Mike did and was greeted by noisy fans who were excited, and probably astonished, to see him leading the pack. Understandably worn from his effort, Mike detoured into a nearby diner and sat down to chat with old friends. It had been the first and last time he would find himself at the front of the Derby pack.

A LITTLE RESPECT

Sportswriters had been making fun of C. C. Pyle's transcontinental foot race ever since he first announced his intention to launch it in early 1927. To them, the idea of running across the country seemed too ridiculous to be taken seriously. Now, as the Derby entered its third and final month, these same critics were probably surprised to find sixty-four runners still getting up each morning to run down the road. In their writing, these reporters revealed a strong bias

MIKE KELLY'S
BUNION DERBY LINIMENT

Used and Recommended by C. C. Pyle and (Red Grange's) 1928 Runners and Trainers of the Famous Los Angeles, to New York Bunion Derby Foot Race, 3422 Miles in 84 days.		Recommended by Trainers & Athletes For Sore Muscles Sprains Stiffness Muscle Cramps Muscle Congestion Strains Charley Horse

RELIEF OR REFUND
PRICE
35¢

MIKE KELLY
Inter-nationally
Known Athlete
and Trainer

Made by Mike Kelly's
BUNION DERBY
PRODUCTS
Goshen, Indiana, U. S. A.

RELIEF OR REFUND
PRICE
35¢

▲ C. C. Pyle might have seen Mike Kelly as a slacker, but Kelly was cut from the same cloth as the Derby director. Kelly was always looking for new ways to get rich and famous. In fact, *Mike Kelly* wasn't even his real name. When Dean Pletcher signed up for the race, he decided a good Irish name would project a better image. After the Derby, the name stuck. During the 1930s, Mike tried to capitalize on his fame (such as it was) by selling Mike Kelly's Bunion Derby Liniment. Apparently, there is no muscle ailment this cream won't cure!

against professional sports and welcomed any sign that the Derby would fail. They seemed especially offended by Pyle's earlier role as an agent. Why, they wondered, should he keep 50 percent of an athlete's pay? What value was he adding by turning sports into entertainment? For these sportswriters, Pyle was still "Cash and Carry," a promoter who turned sports into "a dirty little business run by rogues."

Day	Date	Mileage	Night Control
64	May 6	28	Gary, IN
65	May 7	66	Mishawaka, IN
66	May 8	41	Ligonier, IN
67	May 9	42	Butler, IN
68	May 10	45	Wauseon, OH
69	May 11	65	Fremont, OH
70	May 12	63	Elyria, OH
71	May 13	51	Arrowhead Beach, OH
72	May 14	41	Ashtabula, OH

The sportswriters, especially the syndicated columnist Westbrook Pegler, were out to have their fun at Pyle's expense. At the end of a sarcastic article about the many "creative" ways Charley Pyle made money off his runners, Pegler joked, "He did overlook one thing, I believe. He does not receive 50 per cent of their prize money," which would be quite a feat, since Pyle was the one *paying* the prize money.

Other observers were able to see past Pyle's failings and appreciate the extraordinary achievement of his runners. Though "much fun and ridicule has been poked at C. C. Pyle," wrote one reporter, the men "are now running because they want to finish what they started. . . . The determination of these runners must be admired." No one defended the Derby more passionately than did Will Rogers in his newspaper column. In one edition, he scolded the sportswriters for their sarcasm: "It's all right to kid and call it bunion, but no athlete in any branch of sport could get up every day for three straight months and run 40 to 70 miles a day." He went further: "There is not a golfer who could have stood the same trip in an automobile." And ended with a personal plea: "So be fair and give 'em a break."

Even with Will Rogers's support in the papers, Pyle kept a low profile through the final weeks of the race. Mostly, he rode ahead of the convoy to make arrangements with the upcoming night controls. He smooth-talked several towns into paying the $1,000 fee—he hadn't completely lost his touch—but just as often he left the negotiations with no money at all.

As race director, F. F. Gunn increased the daily average running distance from 38 to 49 miles in Indiana and Ohio and began enforcing the midnight cutoff. When Harry Rea and the injured Olli Wantinnen failed to make the deadline into Mishawaka, Indiana, Grange had to hand them their travel deposits and ask them to leave. These were two men who had consistently been in the top ten of the race and just five days before had tied Johnny Salo for a stage-race victory. Such was the new order under F. F. Gunn: rules were rules. Rea and Wantinnen were sent packing.

RACE WALKERS SURVIVE AND THRIVE

The Derby's race walkers found themselves well represented among the leaders. They had taken it slow over the Derby's hazardous early miles and had survived as so many others dropped out. Then they picked up their pace and thrived as converted runners.

Young Harry Abramowitz of New York City had recently cracked the top ten, while Giusto Umek, the Italian champion, had moved into eighth place. Unexpectedly, on day 69, May 11, in northwestern Ohio, Giusto appeared to give up. For reasons unknown, he sat down on a rock and wouldn't budge, even when his trainers begged and pleaded with him to get up. Finally, in his own good time, Giusto stood—and sprinted to the night control as fast as he ever had.

That same day, Peter Gavuzzi called a halt to his own effort. The liquid diet forced on him by his infected tooth left him too weak to run 50 miles a day. He withdrew from the race, and Phillip Granville, the Jamaican-Canadian race-walker-turned-runner, moved up one position into third place.

RENDEZVOUS IN CLEVELAND

On the evening of May 12, day 70, automobile-factory worker Mike Joyce hitched a ride into Cleveland from the Elyria night control to surprise his family. Back in February, Mike had left his wife and five small children to join Pyle's Derby. He had quit a good-paying factory job, too, all on the slim hope of winning a fortune. Now, walking through his front door, he was so bronzed by the sun, so gritty and tough-looking, his children didn't even recognize him. The littlest ones ran screaming from the room. But his wife packed him a hamper of food to take with him on the road: two dozen eggs, a cake, three roast chickens, and a pound of butter. The next day, as Mike ran through the city, his co-workers in the automobile factory pooled their money and presented him with $100 for expenses. This was a good investment: Mike was running

in fourth place, one behind Phillip and one ahead of Giusto.

Nineteen-year-old Norman Codeluppi was out of contention, but he, too, had a rendezvous with a girl in Cleveland. History doesn't tell us what he said to Mary, his sweetheart, when he met up with her, nor what she said to him. We do know that Norman abandoned his original plan to drop out of the race. His loyalty to the other runners and his determination to finish what he had started had grown too strong. Norman left Mary in Cleveland but vowed to return after reaching New York.

EVERYONE'S WORST FEAR

With 300 miles to go, Andy Payne remarked, "The only thing that can stop me is a car." It was true. On day 71, May 13, Harry Sheare was knocked out of the Derby by a reckless automobile and was fortunate to come away with his life. Several unlucky bunioneers had been struck on the lonely western highways—mostly at night—and now a few more hit-and-runs occurred in the more populated East. Even the late-pack runners, already out of the prize money, feared nothing more than a freak accident to end their bid at crossing the continent. How many of the remaining fifty-five runners would survive to complete their quest?

13
PENNSYLVANIA, NEW YORK, AND NEW JERSEY: THE HOME STRETCH

[Hardrock] Simpson . . . has retained a real smile
throughout the eleven weeks' battle with blisters and
other inconveniences. He seems to regard the whole affair
as something of a lark.
—Washington Post, May 21, 1928

As the Derby reached Erie, Pennsylvania, on day 73, May 15, Andy Payne enjoyed a comfortable 20-hour lead. The last of the Finns, Johnny Salo of Passaic, New Jersey, knew it was too great a lead to overcome, but he intended to make Andy work for his victory nonetheless. He told a reporter, "I may have to be content with second place, but even then I won't growl." For his part, Andy recalled three previous race leaders and what had befallen them: Willie Kolehmainen, the veteran who made the rookie mistake of starting out too fast; Arthur Newton, the greatest distance runner

128

of his generation, who couldn't get over a nagging Achilles heel; and Peter Gavuzzi, the bristle-bearded Britisher who was brought down by an infected tooth, of all things. Andy knew his main goal was to avoid a mistake that could cost him victory—and $25,000.

Day	Date	Mileage	Night Control
73	May 15	46	Erie, PA
74	May 16	60	Jamestown, NY
75	May 17	44	Bradford, PA
76	May 18	50	Wellsville, NY
77	May 19	53	Bath, NY
78	May 20	58	Waverly, NY
79	May 21	75	Deposit, NY
80	May 22	59	Liberty, NY
81	May 23	38	Middletown, NY
82	May 24	38	Suffern, NY
83	May 25	25	Passaic, NJ
84	May 26	12+20	New York, NY

Andy reassured the fans that he wasn't going to "dog it," but he did slow his pace. The 9-to-10-minute miler became an 11-minute miler over the longer stage races in New York State. Johnny cut Andy's lead in slices but never reduced it to less than 15 hours—still more than a half-day cushion. No duel to the finish ever materialized.

Did that mean there was nothing left to root for in the race's final days? Not exactly. A few midpackers, those outside the top ten, put on sterling stage-race performances, none more impressive than Hardrock's on day 78, May 20. He ran the 58 miles into the Waverly, New York, night control, keeping all the other runners at his back. It was his first and only stage-race victory. For a day, at least, it was Hardrock the reporters wanted to talk to. "I do not know whether I'll keep on with pro racing or not," Hardrock told one, adding, "I did my stuff for one day."

"CONCRETE ROLLER COASTER"

Unfortunately, the next day, the city of Binghamton, New York, refused to pay Pyle's fee. So the Derby pressed on to Deposit, New York, where the town leaders were more willing. This made for the longest day of the entire Derby, 75 miles over rolling hills, a regular "concrete roller coaster," as one reporter put it.

Several of the runners were ready to give up. One recalled seeing some of his comrades "laying along side the road with their faces in the grass." Norman Codeluppi broke into tears, thinking he would miss the midnight cutoff and be eliminated so close to New York City. Arthur Newton and Red Grange worked tirelessly to coax the stragglers out of their despair. Arthur had to pull more than one runner to his feet and physically shove him down the road. The kindly South African accompanied the final group into the night control at three o'clock in the morning, just three hours before they were supposed to wake up and do it all over again. Fortunately, Arthur convinced F. F. Gunn to suspend the midnight cutoff rule just one more time. "I couldn't bear to see men, who had already gallantly covered some thousands of miles, drop out when they were so near their goal," he explained. Grange did his part by delaying the next morning's start by an hour.

END OF THE LINE

The Bunion Derby was headed toward an anticlimax. No dramatic finish awaited; the results were already set in stone. As luck would have it, though, Pyle was able to squeeze out one last ballyhoo—

▲ "Hardrock" Simpson hit his stride too late to make
a push for prize money, but not too late to boost his
pride and confidence. After the Derby, Hardrock
kept running both for money and for personal
accomplishment. Every year on his birthday, until he
was into his sixties, Hardrock would run a mile for
every year of his age. "He called it his 'birthday run.'"

➤ Johnny Salo jogs into his hometown, Passaic, New Jersey, accompanied by a trio of policemen on motorcycles, a cyclist, and a caravan of automobiles.

and a little more money—on the second-to-last day of the race. The elected leaders of Passaic, New Jersey, Johnny Salo's hometown, requested the privilege of hosting the Derby on its final night. They didn't need to ask twice. Pyle collected $1,000, and the city set to work planning a celebration for their hometown hero—and on his thirty-fifth birthday, too!

City officials declared May 25 a half holiday in Johnny's honor. Workers took the afternoon off to join the celebration downtown. At a special ceremony, the superintendent of public safety awarded Johnny a position on the Passaic police force. It was a steady job for the unemployed shipyard worker, and it would serve him well after completing the Bunion Derby. "I did it for the wife and kiddies," Johnny declared, meaning his participation in the Derby. He added graciously, "I am proud to run second after Andy. . . . He is a better runner than I am."

All fifty-five runners who had crossed into New York State from Pennsylvania had survived to exit the other side into New Jersey, despite averaging more than 50 miles a day. About a dozen miles to the east, New York's growing skyline lay just out of sight beyond the horizon. The next morning—day 84, May 26—the runners would sleep in and have the full day to themselves. Pyle wanted them rested and scrubbed and shaved for their final showing-off in Madison Square Garden. He planned a 4:00 p.m. start to allow for a prime-time arrival at the Garden. The bunioneers would run a mere 12 miles, the easiest day of the Derby so far.

At least, that's the way it looked on paper.

❶❹
NEW YORK CITY: FINISH LINE

Every man who finishes such a race is a winner.
He has shown strength of heart and purpose,
which should uplift him with pride
and uplift his children after him.
—Ben Richman, brother and trainer of three Bunion Derby runners,
Sam, Arthur, and Morris

The last day was all ceremony, no competition. Everyone knew that Andy Payne, the kid from Foyil, would win the Bunion Derby, even if he had to crawl to the finish. The bunioneers jogged 10 miles to the Hudson River, then were ferried across to Manhattan in a single boat. At the Forty-Second Street pier, they leaped ashore to the cheers of about a hundred well-wishers. Lanes up Tenth Avenue and east on Forty-Ninth Street had been roped off for their benefit. Along the way, cars tooted their horns, police officers blew their whistles, and onlookers clapped their hands.

The runners entered Madison Square Garden and circled the track . . . 200 times! One would think the boys had run far enough, but C. C. Pyle—back in charge of the Derby as the publicity-shy F. F. Gunn lay low—wanted to charge admission one last time. And one last time, the paid attendance was disappointingly small. Just a few hundred spectators were willing to pay the

135

▼ The skyline of New York City in 1931, three years after the end of the Bunion Derby. In 1928, the two tallest buildings, the Chrysler Building (far left) and the Empire State Building (far right), had not yet been built.

Midtown Skyscrapers fr. Weehawken B 5792a Copyright 1932 by Irving Underhill Inc. N.Y.

$1.65 admission. Instead of a crowd, the Garden held a "forest of empty seats," as one reporter wrote. To those who did come in, the hobbling, shuffling runners were "about as inspiring as wet wash on a sagging clothesline," another newspaperman wrote.

After twelve weeks of daily ultramarathons, everyone associated with the Derby had had enough. African American Sammy Robinson told a reporter, "I'm doggoned glad this is . . . over." He added colorfully, "My feet are so hot they burned the blankets last night. When I get back to my home town of Atlantic City I'm going to park little Sammy beside that old ocean and stick my feet in it and say, 'Drink, dogs, drink!'" (In 1928, "dogs" was slang for "feet.") Even Pyle's assistant, Red Grange, admitted, "I was never so tired of anything in my life."

One of the late-pack finishers had a different take: "When you've been through torture like this, it is a dangerous thing to stop the agony all at once. . . . When all the misery's gone you feel kind of lonesome and lost." For his part, Pyle admitted he had lost money, even while promising bigger and better to come: "This country is going marathon mad. . . . There are going to be more marathons . . . and more transcontinental footraces than anybody would have dreamed to be possible."

But first, Pyle had to pay out $48,500 to the top-ten finishers of his race. The sportswriters took advantage of the situation to build some lighthearted suspense: would the prize winners get paid? Pyle did his best to reassure them that they would: "I'll pay the winners off in real money, not buttons," he said. He also announced a special awards ceremony for the following Friday evening—just before the start of a 26-hour running event to which he would, yes, charge admission. Oddly, he added that he was placing the money in the hands of Madison Square Garden event director Tex Rickard.

This may have been Pyle's way of signaling that he did not actually have the Bunion Derby prize money but would rely on the financial backing of a sports promoter even more successful than himself. Twenty years before, while Pyle had been dabbling in vaudeville and the movies, Tex Rickard began single-handedly turning boxing from a low-class racket into a respectable sport. Then he had built a new Madison Square Garden and turned it into America's premier sports palace. Why would Rickard come to Pyle's financial rescue? It's possible that he intervened to avoid the scandal of unpaid debts that would have reflected badly on both him and his beloved Madison Square Garden (also known as "The House That Tex Built").

On the other hand, there is also evidence that F. F. Gunn might have gotten stuck with Pyle's $50,000 tab. Apparently, through some sloppiness on his part, Gunn had accidentally signed a deal that made him an *equal partner* with Pyle and, therefore, equally liable for the debts. Whether it was Rickard or Gunn—or both—Pyle was fortunate to get bailed out at the last minute by at least one millionaire.

Final Standings		Hrs: Mins: Secs
First:	Andy Payne	573:40:13
Second:	Johnny Salo	588:40:13
Third:	Phillip Granville	613:42:30
Fourth:	Mike Joyce	636:43:08
Fifth:	Giusto Umek	641:27:16
Sixth:	William Kerr	641:37:47
Seventh:	Louis Perella	658:45:42
Eighth:	Ed Gardner	659:56:47
Ninth:	Frank Von Flue	681:41:49
Tenth:	John Cronick	681:42:38

A cleaned-up Andy Payne, now appropriately #1, receives his check from the hands of Madison Square Garden's boxing promoter, Tex Rickard. C. C. Pyle, uncharacteristically without a hat, looks on.

At the awards ceremony, Andy Payne received his $25,000, of which he owed 12 percent, or $3,000, to the government as income tax and 10 percent, or $2,500, to his trainer, Tom Young. The remaining $19,500 went to pay off the mortgage on the family farm with enough left over to pay for college and a new automobile. Johnny Salo, the last of the Finns, took $10,000 for second place along with a steady job on the Passaic police force. Phillip Granville, the Jamaican-Canadian race-walk champion, claimed $5,000 for third and summed up his accomplishment memorably to the press: "Lindbergh only sat down and drove an engine for 36 hours. I ran 84 days, on my feet." What's more, Phillip had a newborn awaiting him when he returned home to Hamilton, Ontario. His wife had delivered a baby while he was busy running across the country.

Mike Joyce earned $2,500, which he hoped would make up for abandoning his family for four months. Mike expressed appreciation for Pyle, which was unusual among the derbymen. Mike told him, "You made me famous." Referring to the prize money, he added,

"My five children have nothing to worry about now, and all because of you." Giusto Umek, having converted himself from a walker into a runner, won the fifth spot. William Kerr, having earned a reputation as a capable athlete and—at least with Pyle—as a troublemaker and a leader of the grumblers, took sixth. Both men earned $1,000. Ed Gardner, who went through fourteen pairs of running shoes and won more daily races than any other Derby runner while failing to keep a consistent pace, came in eighth and also claimed $1,000. Harry Abramowitz, struck by shin splints down the stretch, finished one spot out of the money in eleventh place.

Forty-four other Bunion Derby finishers returned home empty-handed. Nineteen-year-old Norman Codeluppi won no prize money, but he did have a girl waiting for him back in Cleveland and a $100 travel deposit to get him there. Tobie Cotton, the fifteen-year-old African American hoping to do something big for his family, finished thirty-fifth and likewise came away with no money. Yet, famed entertainer Bill "Bojangles" Robinson put on a benefit performance in Harlem in behalf of the Cotton family. With the money raised, well-wishers gave a diamond-studded gold medal to Tobie and a new car to the family—with $400 left over to present to Mrs. Cotton back home in California!

Hardrock Simpson finished thirty-sixth, a lot lower down than his fans in North Carolina had hoped but a remarkable accomplishment nonetheless. His feat became a prelude to a lifetime as a distance-runner enthusiast. Meanwhile, "bridge sleeper" Mike Kelly placed where he deserved, in next-to-last place, but he still had an experience few others could boast of.

Arthur Newton, who had dropped out of the race in Arizona but had stuck with the Derby anyway, ended up running about half the final 2,500 remaining miles. As the race's so-called technical

adviser, Arthur had provided the runners with much needed encouragement and advice along the way. In appreciation for his expertise and his care, a group of bunioneers pooled their money to award him a two-handled "loving cup." They understood that, for eighty-four days, they had been in the presence of distance-running greatness and a man of rare generosity.

The fifty-five courageous men who completed the Bunion Derby claimed no greater reward than the ability to say they had done it: crossed the United States on foot in eighty-four days. Until the Bunion Derby, no one had ever contemplated, let alone attempted and completed, such an undertaking. Now here were fifty-five more or less average men who accomplished what few had believed possible. In fact, most Bunion Derby watchers had been convinced it would be positively harmful. Following the race, a team of physicians examined thirty-eight of the runners and found no ill effects to either their hearts or to any other organs. The Bunion Derby pushed back the accepted limits of human athletic endurance.

Would it launch a new distance-running boom in America?

◄ Bill "Bojangles" Robinson grew up with American show business. Before the turn of the twentieth century, he performed for pennies on the side of a minstrel show. After 1900, he went on the vaudeville circuit, first in a comedy duo, then as a tap-dancing virtuoso as one of the first black solo acts. Robinson debuted on Broadway in the spring of 1928, putting him in New York as the Derby caravan pulled into town. Despite his busy stage schedule, Robinson found time to support the cause of Tobie Cotton and his family.

FINISH

CRASH!

One of the most heroic,
if one of the most absurd,
athletic contests ever held.
—Unknown journalist

Not right away.

After reaching New York, Pyle told a reporter that America was on the verge of going "marathon mad" and was "just entering the golden age of the foot." He predicted that soon there would be "hundreds of thousands of distance runners in this country." He acted on this conviction by organizing his "second annual" transcontinental foot race. Incredibly, many of the participants from 1928 came back, including Johnny Salo, Peter Gavuzzi, Ed Gardner, Arthur Newton, Giusto Umek, Phillip Granville, Mike Joyce, Harry Abramowitz, and Hardrock Simpson.

The second annual race was run east to west, from New York City back to Los Angeles, following a more challenging southerly route. This time, Pyle raised the entrance fee to $300 to ensure that only serious runners—no "tourists"—would sign up. Eighty runners toed the starting line in New York, and only nineteen reached the finish line in Los Angeles. All who ran had to cover their own costs. Pyle paid for no food or accommodations.

In 1929, the runners understood better what the race required and had trained more effectively. As a result, their average pace was a full minute-per-mile faster, the winning time almost 60 hours quicker in a race that was more than 100 miles longer. Peter, Ed, and Johnny led the way in the eastern states. (Arthur stayed close but was injured when struck by a car in Illinois.) Ed was forced out by a nagging leg injury, but Peter and Johnny ran together practically step for step the rest of the way across the southwest. The lead changed between them seven times in the final four weeks until, in an exciting finish, the Finnish-American nipped the Italo-Brit by just 2 minutes and 47 seconds! The other 1928 veterans—Giusto, Hardrock, Phillip, Harry, and Mike—all finished in the top ten.

As in 1928, however, Pyle's ultramarathon extravaganza failed to bring in money. Neither Peter nor Johnny nor anyone else received a dime in prizes. C. C. Pyle's luck had plumb run out. "It's no good," he told the winners. "There's no money."

WHAT BECAME OF THE BALLYHOO?

A few months later, in October, the Roaring Twenties came to a "crashing" halt when the New York stock market plunged. Investors lost billions of dollars in one bad week. But worse than that, they lost confidence—and so did their countrymen. Not all at once, but gradually, steadily, Americans stopped believing all the ballyhoo about going faster, higher, farther. The roar became a whimper.

America, and most of the rest of the world, too, entered a decade of hard times we know today as the Great Depression. During the 1930s, Americans generally lived life at a slower pace and in a quieter tone. Oddly, dance marathons—sometimes called "bunion derbies" and sometimes simply "walkathons"—continued into

STAGE · BROADWAY · SCREEN

VARIETY

PRICE 25¢.

Published Weekly at 154 West 46th St., New York, N. Y., by Variety, Inc. Annual subscription, $10. Single copies, 25 cents.
Entered as second-class matter December 22, 1905, at the Post Office at New York, N. Y., under the act of March 3, 1879.

VOL. XCVII. No. 3   NEW YORK, WEDNESDAY, OCTOBER 30, 1929   88 PAGES

WALL ST. LAYS AN EGG

Going Dumb Is Deadly to Hostess In Her Serious Dance Hall Profesh

A hostess at Roseland has her problems. The paid steppers consider their work a definite profession calling for specialized technique and high-power salesmanship.

"You see, you gotta sell your personality," said one. "Each one of we girls has our own clientele to cater to. It's just like selling dresses in a store—you have to know what to sell each particular customer.

"Some want to dance, some want to kid, some want to get soupy, and others are just 'misunderstood husbands'."

Girls applying for hostess jobs at Roseland must be 21 or older. They must work five nights a week. They are strictly on their own, no salary going with the job and the house collecting 18 cents on every 35 cent

DROP IN STOCKS ROPES SHOWMEN

Hunk on Winchell

When the Walter Winchells moved into 204 West 55th street, late last week, June, that's Mrs. Winchell, selected a special room as Walter's exclusive sleep den for his late hour nights. She shussshed the Winchell kidlets when her husband dove in at his usual eight o'clock the first morning.

At noon, Walter's midnight, his sound proof room was penetrated by so many high C's he awoke with but four hours of dreams and a grouch. Investigated at once, after having signed the lease of course.

Many Weep and Call Off Christmas Orders — Legit Shows Hit

MERGERS HALTED

The most dramatic event in the financial history of America is the collapse of the New York Stock Market. The stage was Wall Street, but the onlookers covered the country. Estimates are that 22,000,000 people were in the market at the time.

Tragedy, despair and ruination

Kidding Kissers in Talkers Burns Up Fans of Screen's Best Lovers

Talker Crashes Olympus

Paris, Oct. 29.

Fox "Follies" and the Fox Movietone newsreel are running this week in Athens, Greece, the first sound pictures heard in the birthplace of world culture, and in all Greece, for that matter.

Several weeks ago, Variety's Cairo correspondent cabled that a cinema had been wired in Alexandria, Cleopatra's home town.

Only Sodom and Gomorrah remain to be heard from.

Boys who used to whistle and girls who used to giggle when love scenes were flashed on the screen are in action again. A couple of years ago they began to take the love stuff seriously and desisted, but the talkers are reviving the ha ha for film osculators.

Heavy loving lovers of silent picture days accustomed to charming audiences into spasms of silent ecstasy when kissing the leading lady are getting the bird instead of the heartbeat. The sound accompaniment is making it tough.

Such a picture romancer as John Gilbert is getting laughs in place of the sighs of other days, and the flaps who still think he's grand are getting sore. One little flap had to be quieted by an usher when making a commotion during a Gilbert

▲ The day after Black Tuesday, even New York's weekly entertainment magazine commented on the events in the financial district. Its catchy headline may have captured the moment better—and more memorably— than the headline of any other paper.

the new decade. The ballyhoo was a little more forced, but dance marathons made for relatively inexpensive entertainment and allowed the spectators to feel sorry for someone else for a change.

But Pyle's prediction of a marathon craze did not come to pass. Distance running did not catch on in the 1930s or for the next three decades after that. In 1972, though, Frank Shorter won the Olympic marathon, the first American in sixty-four years to do so. And his feat set off a running boom that has only grown over the past four decades.

By 2015, the growth had started to level off, but the total numbers were still impressive. Eighteen million runners (more than half of them women) entered at least 28,000 different running events in the United States. Over half a million runners finished one or more of 750 marathons, and about 50,000 entered the 1,000-mile-plus ultramarathon races that year. With more than 50 million self-described runners and joggers (about the same number of participants as bowling and double the number of both golfers and basketball players), running has become one of America's most popular participation sports.

For all his ignorance about the physical demands of distance running, C. C. Pyle was exactly right about its future appeal as a participation sport. His mistake in 1928, and again in 1929, was in believing distance running could be made into a moneymaking spectator sport. History has proved him wrong. Today, every year, hundreds of thousands of Americans pay $100 or more to *run* in a marathon, but almost no one pays to *watch* one. As Pyle learned from the Derby's spectators, "You can't charge them anything."

Today's marathoners don't run because some promoter is offering a big cash prize. They run for the exercise or the pure

joy of it (or both). They run to meet new people and travel to new places. Most of all, as the bunioneers discovered in 1928, they run to try to accomplish a challenging goal they have set for themselves. In the twenty-first century, more than eighty years after the Bunion Derby, distance running has become much more about *participation* and much less about *ballyhoo*.

◄ Frank Shorter won the marathon at the 1972 Olympic Games in Munich in 2 hours and 12 minutes. He stayed with the pack for the first third of the race, then took the lead and never gave it up. He ran alone at the front for the final eighteen miles.

▲ Runners in the author's hometown Flying Pig Marathon begin the fourth of twenty-six miles as they cross the Clay Wade Bailey Bridge into Ohio. These midpack runners illustrate how marathon running in the United States has expanded from an elite competition to a mass celebration of athletic participation.

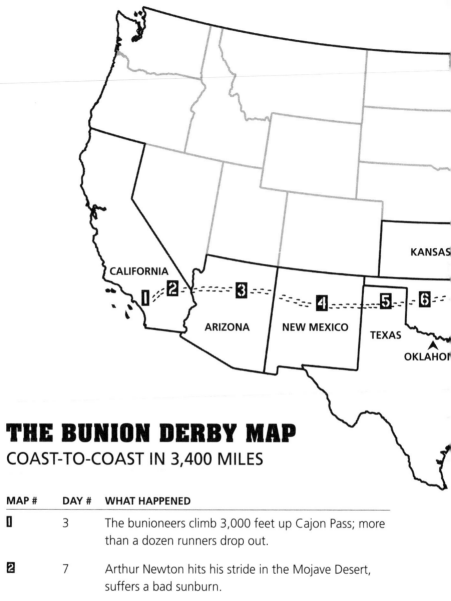

THE BUNION DERBY MAP
COAST-TO-COAST IN 3,400 MILES

MAP #	DAY #	WHAT HAPPENED
1	3	The bunioneers climb 3,000 feet up Cajon Pass; more than a dozen runners drop out.
2	7	Arthur Newton hits his stride in the Mojave Desert, suffers a bad sunburn.
3	17	Andy Payne comes down with tonsillitis, runs through a raging fever.
4	26	Bunion Derby grumblers bring their complaints to C. C. Pyle: poor accommodations and no stage race prize money.
5	33	A blue norther blows snow across the runners' paths; slick mud slows them down.
6	39	Ed Gardner is threatened by a shotgun-toting Oklahoman who dares him to pass a white man.

MAP #	DAY #	WHAT HAPPENED
7	47	Andy Payne and Peter Gavuzzi enter Joplin tied at 295 total hours of running.
8	59	Peter Gavuzzi shaves his bushy beard and angers C. C. Pyle.
9	66	The Derby racers let slacker Mike Kelly run first into his hometown, Goshen, Indiana.
10	71	Harry Sheare is bumped from the race by a car.
11	79	The fifty-five remaining bunioneers complete the longest mileage of the entire race: 75 miles from Waverly to Deposit, New York.
12	83	Johnny Salo receives a hero's welcome—and a job in the police department—from his hometown, Passaic, New Jersey.

SOURCE NOTES*

The source of each quotation in this book is found below. The citation indicates the first words of the quotation and its document source. The document sources are listed either in the bibliography or below.

START (PAGE 8)
"the greatest, most stupendous . . .": Pyle, quoted in Williams, p. 58.

CHAPTER 1 (PAGE 13)
"We are living . . .": Pickens, quoted in Williams, p. 4.
"What for?": Ederle, quoted in Dahlberg, p. 141.

CHAPTER 2 (PAGE 21)
"The American who buys . . .": Pope, quoted in Nevins, p. 256.
"Father of Route 66": Kelly, *Father of Route 66*, p. 4.
"Often you drove . . .": Patrick, p. 216.
"We prefer Sixty Six . . .": Avery, quoted in Kelly, *Father of Route 66*, p. 170.
"speed up construction . . .": John Woodruff, quoted in Ibid, p. 192.
"Put on a foot race!": Ibid, p. 195.
"the P. T. Barnum of professional sports": Wallis, p. 12.

CHAPTER 3 (PAGE 31)
"Money meant nothing . . .": Grange, quoted in Carroll, p. 83.
"the greatest Humbug of them all": Stephens, p. 54.
"putting on . . . glittering appearances . . .": Barnum, quoted in P.T. Barnum, barnum.org/humbugs.html.
"courage, resolution, and endurance": T. Roosevelt, quoted in Zirin, p. 30.
"I'm so dog-tired . . .": Grange, p. 56.

---

*Websites active at time of publication

"How would you like . . .": Grange, p. 91.

"was pretty much of . . .": Halas, quoted in Carroll, p. 102.

"God-given": Ibid, p. 35.

"harmed college football" and "done a disservice": Ibid, p. 101.

"$100,000 football players": Zuppke, quoted in Ibid, p. 99.

"I'm getting it . . .": Grange, quoted in Ibid, p. 114.

"I would have been more popular . . .": Ibid, p. 96.

"wasn't nearly as hard" and "in need of a . . .": Grange, p. 113.

"The fact that people hated . . .": Pyle, quoted in Johnston, p. 34.

"jumps, lunges and wiles": Engelmann, p. 279.

"like a cat walking . . .": Ibid, p. 48.

"a con artist . . ." and "circusing": Reisler, pp. 131, 135.

Origin of the idea for the foot race: "Pedestrians Given a Break," by
Paul Lowry, *Los Angeles Times*, April 27, 1927.

"the greatest race . . .": "Intensive Training," *'Andy' Payne Edition
of the Official Program: C. C. Pyle's First Annual International
Trans-Continental Footrace.*

CHAPTER 4 (PAGE 47)

"Well, if a man enters . . .": Williams, p. 5.

"A Brief History of the Marathon" sidebar: Sears, pp. 36–39.

"beautifully built . . ." and "poetry of motion": Kastner, *Bunion Derby*,
p.139.

"seemed to just glide . . .": Williams, p. 98.

"Here's a chance . . ." and "My wife pushed me . . .": Mabel Gardner
and Ed Gardner, quoted in "Ed Gardner's Wife Has Too Many
Silver Loving Cups," *Black Dispatch* [Oklahoma City, OK], April 19,
1928.

"It's the mortgage . . ." and "I can accomplish . . .": Andy Payne,
quoted in "My Boy 'Andy,'" *'Andy' Payne Edition of the Official
Program. . . .*

CHAPTER 5 (PAGE 60)

"I'm here to say . . .": Oldfield, quoted in Kastner, *Bunion Derby*, p. 76.

"unaware of the magnitude . . ." and "a desperately . . .": Newton, *Running in Three Continents*, p. 93.

"some of the craziest . . .": Simpson, quoted in *Maroon and Gold*, March 1, 1928.

"serve the men . . .": Williams, p. 148.

"the big chef . . . ": "Indians Annex Pyle's Events," by Braven Dyer, *Los Angeles Times*, February 20, 1928.

CHAPTER 6 (PAGE 66)

"Today the eyes of the world . . .": Pyle, quoted in Williams, p. 58.

"You could not raise . . .": Andy Payne, quoted in Kastner, *Bunion Derby*, p. 38.

"fifty miles a day . . .": Kastner, *Bunion Derby*, p. 36.

"land yacht": "Pyle Gives Up $5,000 and Gets Auto Back," *Washington Post*, May 6, 1928.

"only licensed mobile . . .": "KGGM Portable Broadcasting Station," *'Andy' Payne Edition of the Official Program*. . . .

CHAPTER 7 (PAGE 74)

"I have never seen . . .": Simpson, quoted in Williams, p. 88.

"God, it was terrible . . .": Joyce, quoted in Kastner, *Bunion Derby*, p. 46.

"Nice, juicy steaks . . .": Williams, p. 117.

"Did you ever try . . .": John Pederson, quoted in Ibid, p. 119.

CHAPTER 8 (PAGE 82)

"We were always . . .": Newton, *Running in Three Continents*, p. 99.

"We're a queer lot . . .": Williams, p. 63.

"won everything in sight": "Granville May Win Pyle's Run," by Braven Dyer, *Los Angeles Times*, April 1, 1928.

"one of the most perfect . . ." and "relentless, machine-like . . ." and "do no running": Ibid.

"A Brief History of Race Walking" sidebar: Sears, pp. 140–158.

"I go nearly all . . .": Howard, quoted in Sears, p. 153.

"close attention to . . .": "General Information," *'Andy' Payne Edition of the Official Program*. . . .

"We undoubtedly slept . . .": Kastner, "The Hells of the Bunyon Derby," p. 81.

"sleep, eat, and run . . .": Pyle, quoted in Williams, p. 107.

"That boy has guts . . .": Pyle, quoted in Ibid., p. 131.

"This race is doing more . . ." and "Physically, I get . . .": Simpson, quoted in Williams, p. 134.

CHAPTER 9 (PAGE 96)

"I am not thinking much . . .": Gardner, quoted in "Angry Texan Didn't Approve of 'Niggers' in Race," *Black Dispatch* [Oklahoma City, OK], April 19, 1928.

"They ain't got no business . . .": Ibid.

"could not understand . . .": Ibid.

"I mean, I was really . . .": Andy Payne, quoted in Williams, p. 151.

CHAPTER 10 (PAGE 101)

"I realized that this isn't a race . . .": "Loping across Country with Pyle's Runners," by Bill Witt, *Dunkirk* [NY] *Evening Observer*, April 20, 1928.

"the biggest athletes . . ." and "the zaniest sporting . . .": Kelly, *Father of Route 66*, pp. 200–201.

"Andy is hard . . .": "Doc" Payne, quoted in Williams, p. 163.

"Hello, home folks . . .": Andy Payne, quoted in Ibid., p. 167.

"show was a flop . . .": Kastner, *Bunion Derby*, p. 97.

"I felt kind of jealous . . .": Rogers, quoted in Crawford, p. 43.

"Come in first . . .": "El Reno Welcomes Runners with Open Arms," *Black Dispatch* [Oklahoma City, OK], April 19, 1928.

CHAPTER 11 (PAGE 110)

"Every man has a different . . .": *Daily Oklahoman*, quoted in Williams, p. 170.

"bristle-bearded Britisher": "Pyle Derby Lap Is Won by Gavuzzi," *Los Angeles Times*, April 30, 1928.

"What . . . came over . . .": Pyle, quoted in "Barber and Law Spoils Pyle's Day," *Los Angeles Times*, May 3, 1928.

"loose" and "I am not connected . . .": F. F. Gunn, quoted in "Pyle's Runners Near End of Moneyless Rainbow Trail," by Westbrook Pegler, *Chicago Daily Tribune*, May 24, 1928.

CHAPTER 12 (PAGE 120)

"The trouble with Pyle's race . . .": Witt, quoted in Williams, p. 194.

"bridge sleeper": Kastner, *Bunion Derby*, p. 65.

"dirty little business . . .": Carroll, p. 102.

"He did overlook . . .": "Advance Agent of Pyle's Bunion Derby Arrives in Gotham to Steam Up Race," by Westbrook Pegler, *Los Angeles Times*, May 18, 1928.

"much fun and ridicule . . .": Williams, p. 258.

"It's all right to kid . . ." and "There is not . . .": Rogers, quoted in Kastner, *Bunion Derby*, p. 146.

"The only thing . . .": Andy Payne, quoted in Williams, p. 244.

CHAPTER 13 (PAGE 128)

"[Hardrock] Simpson . . . has retained . . .": "Payne in Tie with Salo for Lap," *Washington Post*, May 21, 1928.

"I may have to be content . . .": Salo, quoted in "Bunioneers Nearing Home Goal in East," *Jefferson City* [MO] *Post-Tribune*, May 18, 1928.

"dog it": Andy Payne, quoted in Ibid.

"I do not know . . .": Simpson, quoted in "Payne in Tie with Salo for Lap," *Washington Post*, May 21, 1928.

"concrete roller coaster": "News That Pyle Has Lost $60,000 Invokes Little Sympathy," *Los Angeles Times*, May 25, 1928.

"laying along side . . .": John Stone, quoted in Kastner, "The Hells of the Bunion Derby," p. 86.

"I couldn't bear . . .": Newton, *Running in Three Continents*, p. 110.

"He called it . . .": "I Will Race Anything on Two or Four Legs," *Burlington* [NC] *Times-News*, July 30, 1978.

"I did it for the wife . . ." and "I am proud . . .": Salo, quoted in Kastner, *Bunion Derby*, p. 159.

CHAPTER 14 (PAGE 135)

"Every man who finishes . . .": Richman, quoted in Kastner, *Bunion Derby*, p. 71.

"forest of empty seats": "Payne Runs First in Famous Parade of Broken Arches," *Indianapolis Star*, May 27, 1928.

"about as inspiring . . .": Carroll, p. 151.

"I'm doggoned glad . . .": Robinson, quoted in "End at Garden Tonight," by James L. Kilgallen, *Syracuse* [NY] *Journal*, May 26, 1928.

"I was never so tired . . .": Grange, quoted in Williams, p. 269.

"When you've been through . . .": "Pyle Sees Fortune in Derby Chiropody," *New York Times*, May 28, 1928.

"This country is going . . .": Pyle, quoted in Ibid.

"I'll pay the winners . . .": Pyle, quoted in "Bunioneer Strike Is Averted," *Syracuse* [NY] *Herald*, May 25, 1928.

"Lindbergh only sat . . .": Granville, quoted in "Cheer Up Folks, Mr. Pyle's Leg Derby May Show Profit," by Westbrook Pegler, *Chicago Daily Tribune*, May 28, 1928.

"You made me . . .": Joyce, quoted in Williams, p. 285.

FINISH (PAGE 144)

"One of the most heroic . . .": Crawford, p. 45.

"marathon mad" and "just entering the golden age . . ." and "hundreds of thousands . . .": Pyle, quoted in Reisler, pp. 5–6.

"It's no good . . .": Pyle, quoted in Kastner, *The 1929 Bunion Derby*, p. 176.

"You can't charge . . .": Pyle, quoted in Williams, p. 207.

BIBLIOGRAPHY*

THE ERA

Aycock, Colleen, and Mark Scott. *Tex Rickard: Boxing's Greatest Promoter*. Jefferson, NC: McFarland, 2012.

Becker, Paula. "Dance Marathons of the 1920s and 1930s." HistoryLink.org, August 25, 2003. historylink.org/index. cfm?DisplayPage=output.cfm&file_id=5534.

Carroll, John M. *Red Grange and the Rise of Modern Football*. Urbana: University of Illinois Press, 1999.

Dahlberg, Tim. *America's Girl: The Incredible Story of How Swimmer Gertrude Ederle Changed the Nation*. With Mary Ederle Ward and Brenda Greene. New York: St. Martin's Press, 2009.

Engelmann, Larry. *The Goddess and the American Girl: The Story of Suzanne Lenglen and Helen Wills*. New York: Oxford University Press, 1988.

Grange, Red. The Red Grange Story: An Autobiography As Told to Ira Morton. Urbana: University of Illinois Press, 1993. First published 1953 by Putnam.

Johnston, Alva. "Profiles: Cash and Carry." *The New Yorker*, December 8, 1928, pp. 31–35. newyorker.com/ magazine/1928/12/08/cash-and-carry.

Kelly, Susan Croce. *Father of Route 66: The Story of Cy Avery*. Norman: University of Oklahoma Press, 2014.

*Websites active at time of publication

Kelly, Susan Croce, and Quinta Scott. *Route 66: The Highway and Its People*. Norman: University of Oklahoma Press, 1988.

Kyvig, David E. *Daily Life in the United States, 1920–1940: How Americans Lived through the "Roaring Twenties" and the Great Depression*. Chicago: Ivan R. Dee, 2004.

Leinwand, Gerald. *1927: High Tide of the 1920s*. New York: Four Walls Eight Windows, 2001.

Martin, Carol J. *Dance Marathons: Performing American Culture in the 1920s and 1930s*. Jackson: University Press of Mississippi, 1994.

Miller, Nathan. *New World Coming: The 1920s and the Making of Modern America*. Cambridge, MA: Da Capo Press, 2003.

Neft, David S., and Richard M. Cohen. *The Football Encyclopedia: The Complete History of Professional NFL Football from 1892 to the Present*. New York: St. Martin's Press, 1991.

Nevins, Allan. *Ford: The Times, the Man, the Company*. New York: Scribner, 1954.

Patrick, Richard K. *Someday It Will Be a Hundred Years Ago*. Printed by the author, 1970.

Pisano, Dominick A., and F. Robert van der Linden. *Charles Lindbergh and the* Spirit of St. Louis. New York: Harry N. Abrams / Smithsonian National Air and Space Museum, 2002.

Rader, Benjamin G. *American Sports: From the Age of Folk Games to the Age of Spectators*. Englewood Cliffs, NJ: Prentice-Hall, 1983.

Reisler, Jim. *Cash and Carry: The Spectacular Rise and Hard Fall of C. C. Pyle, America's First Sports Agent.* Jefferson, NC: McFarland, 2009.

Robinson, Ray. *American Original: A Life of Will Rogers.* New York: Oxford University Press, 1996.

St. James. "1920s Entertainment Flagpole-Sitting." HubPages, March 16, 2009. st-james.hubpages.com.

Stephens, Henry L. "The Humbug." In *The Comic Natural History of the Human Race.* Philadelphia: S. Robinson, 1851, pp. 49–54.

Wallis, Michael. *Route 66: The Mother Road.* New York: St. Martin's Press, 1990.

Zirin, Dave. *A People's History of Sports in the United States: 250 Years of Politics, Protest, People, and Play.* New York: New Press, 2008.

RUNNERS, RUNNING, AND THE BUNION DERBY

"Andy Payne" Edition of the Official Program: C. C. Pyle's First Annual *International Trans-continental Footrace.* Courtesy of Canadian County Historical Museum, El Reno, Oklahoma.

Bigbee, Dan, and Lily Shangreaux. *The Great American Footrace.* San Francisco: Independent Television Service, 2002. (DVD).

———. *The Great American Footrace.* archive.itvs.org/footrace/index.htm, 2002.

Crawford, Bill. "The Bunion Derby." *Oklahoma Today.* May–June 1998: pp. 38–45.

Derderian, Tom. *The Boston Marathon: A Century of Blood, Sweat, and Cheers.* Chicago: Triumph Books, 2003.

———. *Boston Marathon: The First Century of the World's Premier Running Event.* Champaign, IL: Human Kinetics, 1996.

Hadgraft, Rob. *Tea with Mr Newton: 100,000 Miles: The Longest 'Protest March' in History.* Southend-on-Sea, UK: Desert Island Books, 2010.

Kastner, Charles B. *Bunion Derby: The 1928 Footrace across America.* Albuquerque: University of New Mexico Press, 2007.

———. "The Hells of the Bunion Derby." *Marathon and Beyond.* July–August 2009, pp. 74–91.

———. "The 1928 Bunion Derby: America's Brush with Integrated Sports." BlackPast.org. blackpast.org/perspectives/1928-bunion-derby-america-s-brush-integrated-sports.

———. *The 1929 Bunion Derby: Johnny Salo and the Great Footrace across America.* Syracuse, NY: Syracuse University Press, 2014.

Lovett, Charlie. *Olympic Marathon: A Centennial History of the Games' Most Storied Race.* Westport, CT: Praeger, 1997.

Lutz, Dick, and Mary Lutz. *The Running Indians: The Tarahumara of Mexico.* Salem, OR: Dimi Press, 1989.

McDougall, Christopher. *Born to Run: A Hidden Tribe, Superathletes, and the Greatest Race the World Has Never Seen.* New York: Vintage Books, 2009.

Newton, Arthur F. H. *Running.* London: H. F. & G. Witherby, 1935.

———. *Running in Three Continents*. London: H. F. & G. Witherby, 1940.

Sears, Edward S. *Running through the Ages*. Jefferson, NC: McFarland, 2001.

Stipp, David. "All Men Can't Jump." Slate.com, June 4, 2012. slate.com/articles/sports/sports_nut/2012/06/long_distance_ running_and_evolution_why_humans_can_outrun_horses_but_ can_t_jump_higher_than_cats_.html.

Williams, Geoff. *C. C. Pyle's Amazing Foot Race: The True Story of the 1928 Coast-to-Coast Run across America*. Emmaus, PA: Rodale Books, 2007.

BOOKS FOR YOUNG READERS

Adler, David A. *America's Champion Swimmer: Gertrude Ederle*. Illustrated by Terry Widener. New York: Gulliver Books, 2000.

Bennett, Cathereen L. *Will Rogers: Quotable Cowboy*. Minneapolis: Runestone Press, 1995.

Bobek, Milan. *1920s: Decades of the 20th Century*. Prescott, AZ: Eldorado Ink, 2005.

Burleigh, Robert. *Flight: The Journey of Charles Lindbergh*. Illustrated by Mike Wimmer. New York: Philomel, 1991.

Fleming, Candace. *The Great and Only Barnum: The Tremendous, Stupendous Life of Showman P. T. Barnum*. Illustrated by Ray Fenwick. New York: Schwartz and Wade Books, 2009.

Griffis, Molly Levite. *The Great American Bunion Derby*. Austin, TX: Eakin Press, 2003.

King, David C. *Al Capone and the Roaring Twenties*. Woodbridge, CT: Blackbirch Press, 1999.

Krull, Kathleen. *Lives of the Athletes: Thrills, Spills (and What the Neighbors Thought)*. Illustrated by Kathryn Hewitt. San Diego: Harcourt, Brace, 1997.

Reynolds, Susan. *The First Marathon: The Legend of Pheidippides*. Illustrated by Daniel Minter. Morton Grove, IL: Albert Whitman, 2006.

NEWSPAPERS AND PERIODICALS

The author found most newspaper coverage of the Bunion Derby in the *Los Angeles Times*, followed by the *Washington Post*, *Chicago Daily Tribune*, and the *New York Times*. Other newspapers provided at least some information on the progress of the race and occasionally some useful quotations.

Amarillo [TX] *Globe-Times*
Arizona Daily Sun [Flagstaff, AZ]
Black Dispatch [Oklahoma City, OK]
Brainerd [MN] *Daily Dispatch*
Brooklyn [NY] *Daily Eagle*
Buffalo [NY] *Courier-Express*
Burlington [NC] *Times-News*
Chicago Defender
Decatur [IL] *Herald*
Dunkirk [NY] *Observer*
Elmira [NY] *Star-Gazette*

El Paso [TX] *Evening Post*

Hartford [CT] *Courant*

Hornell [NY] *Tribune-Times*

Huntington [IN] *Herald*

Indianapolis News

Indianapolis Star

Jamestown [NY] *Evening Journal (*and *Morning Post)*

Jefferson City [MO] *Post-Tribune*

Joplin [MO] *Globe*

Kane [PA] *Republican*

Lincoln [NE] *Star*

Maroon & Gold [Elon University, NC]

Morning Herald [Gloversville, NY]

Nassau Daily Review [Freeport, NY]

New York [NY] *Age*

Ogden Standard-Examiner [Ogden City, UT]

Olean [NY] *Times Herald*

Oxnard [CA] *Daily Journal*

Rochester [NY] *Democrat and Chronicle*

San Bernardino County [CA] *Sun*

Springfield [MO] *Leader*

St. Louis Post-Dispatch

Syracuse [NY] *Herald*

Syracuse [NY] *Journal*

ADDITIONAL WEBSITES

DATA ON RUNNERS AND RUNNING
IN THE TWENTY-FIRST CENTURY

"2015 State of the Sport—U.S. Race Trends." Running USA.
runningusa.org/2015-state-of-sport-us-trends

"2012 Sports, Fitness and Leisure Activities Topline Participation
Report," sponsored by the Sporting Goods Manufacturers
Association.
assets.usta.com/assets/1/15/SGMA_Research_2012_Participation_
Topline_Report.pdf

Marathon Statistics.
FindMyMarathon.com.
findmymarathon.com/statistics.php

"Age an Asset for Ultramarathon Runners, Study Suggests" by Kim
Painter, January 9, 2014.
USA Today.
usatoday.com/story/news/nation/2014/01/08/ultramarathon-age-
study/4374867/

THE HISTORY OF RUNNING
AND RACE WALKING

"The Battle of Marathon, 490 BC," 2006.
EyeWitness to History.
eyewitnesstohistory.com/marathon.htm

International Association of Athletics Federations.
iaaf.org/disciplines/race-walks/20-kilometres-race-walk

"An Illustrated History of Race Walking" by Mike Rosenbaum.
About Sports/About.com.
trackandfield.about.com/od/distanceevents/ss/illusracewalk.htm

"The History of Race Walking" by Jeff Salvage.
Active.com.
active.com/walking/articles/the-history-of-race-walking-870430

HISTORICAL DATA

"Legal Immigration to the United States, 1820–2014."
Migration Policy Institute.
migrationpolicy.org/programs/data-hub/us-immigration-trends

"Segregation Was the Rule in 1928."
International Swimming Hall of Fame.
ishof.org/assets/segregation-in-swimming-was-the-rule-in-1928.pdf

"The Rise of the Klan in Texas, 1920–1930" by Bob Feldman,
December 12, 2012.
The Rag Blog.
theragblog.com/bob-feldman-the-rise-of-the-klan-in-texas-1920-1930/

ACKNOWLEDGMENTS

This book could not have been written without the work of Charles Kastner and Geoff Williams. Their 2007 books on the Bunion Derby caught the attention of *Runner's World*, whose feature article on the event sparked my imagination. As I set about researching and writing this surprising story for middle-grade readers, I was the lucky beneficiary of not one but *two* recently published books as sources. Just as important, both authors were generous with their time in responding to my many e-mailed questions and for agreeing to read my manuscript. (Particular thanks to Charles Kastner for his especially detailed feedback.) I am extremely grateful to both authors.

Several library archivists helped me bring this book to its final state and deserve special mention: Penny Beals of the El Reno (Oklahoma) Carnegie Library for allowing the use of the archives' essential Derby photos; Patty Reuter of the Canadian County (Oklahoma) Historical Museum for photocopying the Bunion Derby program that I might otherwise have missed; Barbara Cessna of the Fenton History Center in Jamestown, New York, for sharing a New York State newspaper search tool that gave me access to many Derby-related newspaper articles; Lasse Teeriaho of the office of the Consulate General of Finland, New York City, for his generosity at the start of my research; Shaunta Alvarez of the Carol Grotnes Belk Library, Elon University, for filling with the greatest dispatch all my requests (and more) about Hardrock Simpson; Sheena Perez of the Oklahoma State University–Tulsa Library for her equally prompt ability to obtain a Cyrus Avery photograph (and Susan Croce Kelly for putting me in touch with her); Earlene Nofziger of the Goshen (Indiana) Historical Society for the Mike Kelly advertisement; Andrea Dunn of the Williams Public Library for the photograph of Andy Payne in Arizona; Lynne Galia at Kraft Foods for the image of the Maxwell House coffeepot-on-wheels; and Passaic City historian Mark Auerbach for sharing his Johnny Salo photograph, official program cover, and several other images I was unable to use. He was especially generous with his time and expertise.

The Public Library of Cincinnati and Hamilton County is one of the jewels of our nation's library systems. My special thanks go to Mary Sanker and her staff at the Mariemont branch library in Cincinnati for shelving my weekly book requests and for their unfailingly cheerful service. I am also grateful to Mark Leja at the main branch for so capably filling my many interlibrary loan requests.

Several editors have helped me bring this book to fruition. Kendra Marcus took an interest in an early draft and suggested that I rework it. Catherine Frank showed careful attention to detail and reliable judgment while guiding me to a much-improved fourth draft. Most of all, Carolyn P. Yoder had the courage to contract a first-time author. She read my drafts with a keen eye and a respect that other authors can only envy. With admirable patience, she nudged me away from rookie mistakes and steered me toward a manuscript I could be proud of.

Joan Hyman performed a most thorough copyedit of my manuscript and verification of my facts and sources. I was fortunate to have her working on my manuscript. Juanita Galuska guided me through the ins and outs of photographic rights and permissions. She showed great patience throughout. Barbara

Grzeslo created a fine final product that is exciting to look at. Her work will surely attract young readers to pick up the book.

Finally, I must acknowledge the unwavering support of my family. Above all, my wife, Sue, has made my work possible. She paid most of the bills during the past six years and never begrudged my unpaid researching-and-writing habit. She maintained her confidence in me even when no light glimmered at the end of the tunnel.

Thank you, Sue.

—AS

INDEX

173

PICTURE CREDITS